DAO DE JING

. . . . .

A

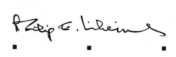

. BOOK

The Philip E. Lilienthal imprint
honors special books
in commemoration of a man whose work
at the University of California Press from 1954 to 1979
was marked by dedication to young authors
and to high standards in the field of Asian Studies.
Friends, family, authors, and foundations have together
endowed the Lilienthal Fund, which enables the Press
to publish under this imprint selected books
in a way that reflects the taste and judgment
of a great and beloved editor.

DAO DE JING

The Book of the Way

LAOZI

Translation and Commentary by

MOSS ROBERTS

UNIVERSITY OF CALIFORNIA PRESS

Berkeley · Los Angeles · London

University of California Press
Berkeley and Los Angeles, California

University of California Press, Ltd.
London, England

First paperback printing 2004

Library of Congress Cataloging-in-Publication Data

Roberts, Moss, 1937–
Dao de jing : the book of the way / translation and
commentary by Moss Roberts.
    p.   cm.
ISBN 0-520-24221-1 (pbk : alk. paper)
1. Laozi. Dao de jing.   I. Laozi. Dao de jing. English.
II. Title.
BL1900.L35 R628   2001
2998.51482—dc21   2001005077

Manufactured in the United States of America

11   10   09   08   07   06   05   04
10   9   8   7   6   5   4   3   2   1

The paper used in this publication meets the minimum
requirements of ANSI / NISO Z39.48-1992 (R 1997)
(*Permanence of Paper*). ∞

DEDICATION AND
ACKNOWLEDGMENTS

IT WAS THE LATE Professor C. N. Tay who suggested that I try my hand at a translation of the *Dao De Jing*. Professor Tay was a friend, a colleague, and a mentor, and I was enthusiastic at the prospect of working with him on this project. Suddenly, on Easter Sunday 1994, Professor Tay passed away. Work on the project had hardly begun; my hopes for a sustained collaboration vanished. I resolved to continue with the translation, in part as a mark of my respect for his memory.

Other unexpected and keenly felt personal losses soon followed. Professor Eric Holtzman died that same month, and then in January of the following year Professor Bernard Fields, a friend since high school, passed away. Another close friend, Leo Cawley, a Vietnam veteran, had died of bone cancer at the age of forty-seven in 1991.

Three variants of the *Dao De Jing* have been found buried in tombs: the Guodian text in a Warring States tomb dated to about 300 B.C., and in a Han tomb at Mawangdui, two texts that date to about 200 B.C. The version published by Fu Yi, a scholar of the Tang period, is also based on a Han tomb text. It is likely that more *Dao De Jing* manuscripts will be excavated. At whose behest was the *Dao De Jing* buried, and with what thought in mind? Was it intended as a comfort to the dead? A spiritual companion among the more practical and ornamental grave goods usually found? Was it seen as a work devoted to the fecund earth mother, which creates all living things and receives them again? Or was the text entombed as a consolation for the living, its meditations on mortality and time and on the passage from shadow to light to shadow (and to the light again?) serving as a bridge to the other realm?

Working on the translation became for me a way of keeping close to lost friends whose companionship I had shared over the better part of a lifetime. In 1999, another noted scholar, John S. Service, passed away. I was privileged to have had a warm relationship with him in the last decade of his life, and I benefited from his thoughtful observations on China and on America. It is to these five friends and scholars that this translation is dedicated.

In 1993, about the time I began thinking about how to approach this project, the Warring States Working Group was getting organized under the leadership of the research team of Professor E. Bruce Brooks and Taeko Brooks. These two scholars had been studying and analyzing the entire Warring States corpus for several decades. With the collaboration of Professor Alvin Cohen at the University of Massachusetts at Amherst, the Brookses summoned into being a new and exciting regional symposium on a wealth of topics relevant to the history of Warring States texts. The group provided a much-needed focus for research work and free-wheeling discussion and has now become an important national and international forum. I was fortunate to have been present at the creation of the group and to have participated in many of its meetings and other activities, and my association with it was quite helpful to my research. I would also like to express appreciation for the indirect but significant contribution of my colleagues at New York University. The senior and junior scholars in our East Asian program have created an intellectual environment that I have found stimulating. Their generous collegiality and energizing spirit of free inquiry have often lifted my own spirits; but beyond that, they have served as a trustworthy point of reference against which to correct one's angle of vision on a wide range of questions. Many a time they have made me think again.

Another person I would like to thank is Professor Fang Ping. In the fall of 1995 I spent a semester at Shanghai Teachers University teaching English. During that time I was fortunate to make the acquaintance of Professor Fang, who is the main living translator of Shakespeare into Chinese. I would like to thank him for reading over a number of my stanzas and for his valuable suggestions on interpretation and style.

My thanks go to my two editors at University of California Press. Doug Abrams encouraged me to pursue this project and spent countless hours trying to put my drafts into presentable shape and discussing with me strategies for the introduction and the translation. His faith in the outcome has been in constant conflict with my own skepticism. Reed Malcolm has skillfully guided the manuscript through its later stages. Carolyn Bond's careful copyediting caught many minor errors, and I thank her for that. But more importantly, she acted as a conscientious and constructive colleague: her persistent and pointed queries often prompted me to rethink and rewrite parts of the translation and the critical apparatus.

My final word of appreciation is to my family: my wife, Florence, whose untiring service as an attorney for the poorer citizens of New York City sustains my faith in human decency, and our children, Sean and Jenny, who have followed her example and in so doing set an example of their own.

CONTENTS

INTRODUCTION

Moss Roberts

THE POEMS AND SAYINGS of the mysterious book of wisdom called *Dao De Jing* have powerfully affected many aspects of Chinese philosophy, culture, and society. In the realm of aesthetics the idea of *Dao,* or the Way, a transcendent natural principle working through all things, has inspired artists and poets who have sought to represent nature in its raw wholeness or have depicted vast landscapes within which human structures and pathways, overwhelmed by mists, mountain faces, and water vistas, hold a tiny and precarious place. With regard to personal spiritual cultivation Daoism offers techniques of concentration and self-control, while in the realm of physiology the Daoist theory of natural cycles points toward systems of internal circulation and techniques of rejuvenation.[1] In its ethical application Daoism teaches self-subordination and frugality and warns of the self-defeating consequences of assertiveness and aggrandizement, whether political, military, or personal.

In the realm of governance political theorists influenced by Laozi have advocated humility in leadership and a restrained and concessive approach to statecraft, either for ethical and pacifist reasons or for tactical ends. The well-known line that opens stanza 60, "Rule a great state as you cook a small fish," has been used in China and in the West as an argument for a "light touch" in governing: the Way creates sufficient order. In a different political context, one mediated by legalist theories of government, a transcendent Way has served to legitimate state builders in constructing impersonal institutions and formulating all-powerful laws. Indeed the marriage of the Way with law *(fa)* is one of the earliest transformations and adaptations of Laozi's thought.[2] On the popular level, by contrast, various anti-authoritarian movements have embraced the *Dao De Jing*'s teachings on the power of the weak.

Thus the *Dao De Jing*, in the world of philosophy a small kingdom in its own right, has spawned diverse schools of thought, and these have elaborated upon and spread widely the original teachings— often in ways that might have surprised or distressed their creator.

The *Dao De Jing* has so wide a compass that it is difficult to think of a comparable work in the Western canon. Passages on nature's patterns of motion and their indifference to man's purposes may evoke for a Western reader themes and language found in Lucretius and his model, Epicurus. If some stanzas concerning statecraft and tactical maneuver suggest Machiavelli, others suggest Gandhi, who personified in his leadership principled humility, minimal struggle, and simplicity of lifestyle. For some readers Laozi's aphorisms and resigned reflections on human life may evoke lines in Ecclesiastes or Proverbs. Comparisons have also been made with Thoreau's warnings about economic overdevelopment and government.

With so many English versions of the *Dao De Jing*, why another? There is much of value in most of the English translations, but each is only partially successful. The synergy of the work's themes as well as the concision of its phrasing make many of its stanzas so ambiguous and suggestive that definitive interpretation, much less translation, has often proved unattainable. Rendering in another language a work that says so much in so few words, and about whose meanings scholars differ greatly, can only be problematic. Even in Chinese, many *Dao De Jing* passages seem like paintings of striking detail that compel the gaze but always remain partly out of focus. Each translator tries to refine the images or to find fresh language to capture the power of Laozi's gnomic lines. In the end, however, the only justification I can offer for a new attempt is that it is meant not only to improve but also to be improved upon. The cumulative effect of multiple translations contributes to the understanding of the *Laozi*, just as the ongoing performance tradition of musical works yields new possibilities of expression and appreciation.

What this version seeks is, first, to bring out the *Dao De Jing*'s political and polemical purposes by situating it in the context of the philosophical debates that raged from the time of Confucius down to the unification of the empire in 221 B.C. Second, it attempts to reproduce the condensed aphoristic force of Laozi's style, the appeal of his intriguing and often indeterminate syntax, and the prevalence of rhymed verse in his original. Unlike most translators, I have avoided relying on prose. Third, in the comments and notes to the stanzas I have included material from recently discovered texts—the two Mawangdui versions, which were published in 1973, and the Guodian version, published in 1998. In this way the reader can learn something about the differences between versions of the text and weigh for himself or herself the significance of the variations in wording and, perhaps more importantly, the differences in the actual number and sequence of the stanzas.[3]

For example, according to the research of one of the leading contemporary Laozi scholars, Yin Zhenhuan, it is likely that the true number of individual stanzas is not eighty-one but as many as 112, some of which, like passages in the *Analects,* are only four or eight words long.[4] For convenience of reference and for the sake of continuity, however, the traditional order of eighty-one is followed in this translation. Ornaments indicate probable stanza divisions within a conventional stanza.

TITLES AND TEXTS

The title *Dao De Jing* may be translated "Canonical text *(jing)* on the Way *(Dao)* and virtue *(de)*." But this now-universal title did not become widely used until the Tang dynasty (A.D. 618–905), when Laozi was officially regarded as a divine guardian of the dynasty. *Laozi* is the older title, going back almost to the creation of the text. Although scholars now generally use the two titles interchangeably, *Dao De Jing* suggests an established classic in the Chinese philosophical tradition, while *Laozi* is more modest—"the words of Master Lao," perhaps. Like the *Mozi,* the *Guanzi,* the *Mencius,* and other titles for writings and records collected under the name of a central figure, *Laozi* suggests a historical document and its original context rather than a canonical work. To reflect the difference between the two titles, in the present work *Dao De Jing* is more frequently, albeit not exclusively, used in the introduction, and *Laozi* in the comments. It is an open question how pleased the self-effacing Laozi would have been to see his little book classified as a *jing*—or for that matter himself as a divinity.

The *Dao De Jing* has come down to us in eighty-one stanzas, a form set slightly before the Christian era began; stanzas 1–37 constitute the first half, stanzas 38–81 the second. Although there are several versions, they are not dramatically different from one another. Two of the versions are named after their scholarly annotators, the Heshang gong *Laozi* and the Wang Bi *Laozi*. A third, the Fu Yi *Laozi*, is named for the Tang-dynasty Daoist scholar who published a text unearthed in A.D. 574 from a Han tomb dating from about 200 B.C.[5] Present-day scholars usually call the current common text the "received text" to distinguish it from recently discovered manuscripts.

The first of these new discoveries was made in 1973 at Mawangdui in the tomb of an official's son; that tomb has been dated to 168 B.C. The Mawangdui *Laozi* was published in 1976. Inscribed on silk, it consists of two texts, A and B, the former dating from about 205–190 B.C., the latter slightly later. These two texts differ from the received version in significant details, but the only major structural difference is that they begin with chapter 38 and end with chapter 37. In other words, the second half of the text comes before the first. Found together with *Laozi* A and B was a rich trove of political and cosmological documents that have been called the *Huangdi sijing,* or the *Four Classics of the Yellow Emperor.*[6]

The Guodian *Laozi,* inscribed on bamboo slips, was found in 1993 and published in 1998.[7] The text was unearthed from a royal tutor's tomb at Guodian, near the city of Ying, the capital of the southern kingdom of Chu. This area contains many graves, and fresh discoveries can be expected. Like the Mawangdui *Laozi,* the Guodian *Laozi* was found as part of a trove of related works of politics and cosmology. All of them are works of established importance and so were probably written well before the time of their burial, approximately 300 B.C. (No complete translation of the accompanying documents has appeared so far.)

The Guodian *Laozi* consists of only about two thousand characters, or 40 percent of the received version, covering in their entirety or in part only thirty-one of the received text's stanzas. The order of the stanzas is utterly different from any later versions. Moreover, it is yet to be determined whether the Guodian *Laozi* represents a sample taken from a larger *Laozi* or is the nucleus of a later five-thousand-character *Laozi*. A current working hypothesis is that the Guodian *Laozi* should be attributed to Laozi, also called Lao Dan, a contemporary of Confucius who may have outlived him, and that the remainder, the non-Guodian text, was the work of an archivist and dates from around 375 B.C.[8]

Let us leave the recent manuscript discoveries and turn to information on the *Dao De Jing* in texts long available. Most traditional Chinese scholars (and a number of modern ones as well) have held that the *Laozi* reflects substantially the time of Confucius, that is, the late sixth or early fifth century B.C., acknowledging occasional interpolations to account for anachronistic language suggesting a somewhat later period. Before the Guodian finds, many modern Chinese and Western scholars argued for a date ranging from the early fourth to the late third century B.C. because sightings of a *Laozi* in Chinese works of the third century B.C. are so fragmentary. One finds lines or partial stanzas, the authorship of which either is not indicated or is attributed to someone named Lao or Lao Dan; but this attribution is not systematic. The *Zhuangzi*, for example, is a Daoist text of the late fourth to early third century B.C. collected under the name of the philosophical recluse Zhuangzi. This work contains several *Dao De Jing* lines or partial stanzas. Sometimes these are attributed to Lao Dan, yet sometimes these quotations from Lao Dan say things that are not in the *Laozi*, though they are compatible with its ideas.

In the *Zhuangzi* and other contemporary texts we find references to the *Shi,* the Odes (later the *Shijing*), and the *Shu,* the Documents (later the *Shujing*), suggesting that these are titles for bodies of shorter works. But it is only in the *Han Feizi,* a compilation of writings on law and statecraft attributed to diplomat and strategist Han Feizi of the late third century B.C., that references to Laozi's work suggest a substantial text; that is, the *Han Feizi* includes some *Dao De Jing* stanzas that are more or less complete. Han Feizi was influenced by Laozi, and he analyzes a number of stanzas in two of his chapters, "Jie Lao" and "Yu Lao." Han Feizi's discussion of stanza 38, for example, opens the "Jie Lao." It was the absence of references to a recognizable oeuvre, *Dao De Jing,* prior to the *Han Feizi* that led many modern scholars, Chinese and Western, to conclude that the work took shape closer to the time of Han Feizi than to the time of Confucius. The Guodian finds of course suggest the opposite.

In the Han period (206 B.C.–A.D. 220) the writings attributed to Laozi were referred to as the *Daode,* the *Laozi,* or the *Laozi jing. Dao* and *de* refer of course to two of the work's primary philosophical terms, the former belonging to the cosmic realm, the latter to the human. But *Dao* and *de* also refer to the two roughly equal sections of the text as it has come down to us: the *Dao* stanzas and the *de* stanzas. The first part of this text (stanzas 1–37) begins with a stanza devoted to *Dao;* the second part (stanzas 38–81) begins with a stanza devoted to *de*. According to one recent study, "the present eighty-one chapters were determined around 50 B.C." in order to make a "perfect number" of nine times nine.[9] The oldest complete *Laozi,* the two Mawangdui texts, dating from about 200 B.C., closely resemble the received version, though neither one has numbered stanzas and both start with the *de,* or second, half (stanzas 38–81).[10] Either this was the original order, or the *de* part became a text before the *Dao* part. The priority of the *de* stanzas had been suspected because the "Jie Lao" begins with stanza 38, and also because Wang Bi's (A.D. 226–249) edition appends to stanza 38 a lengthy annotation that is virtually an introduction. Against this hypothesis stands the fact that about half of the Guodian *Laozi* consists of *Dao* stanzas, half of *de* stanzas.

It is not possible to say when the *Dao* section was placed before the *de* section. In his joint biography of Laozi and Han Feizi in the *Shiji* (*Records of the Historian,* a general history completed about 90 B.C.), renowned Han historian Sima Qian (145 – 86? B.C.) refers to a five-thousand-word text devoted to the theme of *Daode*. But did Sima Qian see a text with the *Dao* stanzas coming first, or is he using the terms *Dao* and *de* in the order of their importance? *Dao* is of course the leading term and *de* must follow in its path; the words are not found transposed. The political philosopher Yan Zun (fl. 53 – 24 B.C.) used *Daode* in the title of his commentary *Daode zhigui,* of which only the *de* section survives. The philosopher Ho Yan (d. 249 A.D.) wrote a *Daode lun*. So the phrase *Daode* (still today a common term for "morality") had title status for the text.

The present form of the Heshang gong commentary has the *Dao* stanzas first and seems to have been divided into a *Daojing* and a *Dejing,* but conjectures on the date of this important early commentary range from the reign of Emperor Wen of the Han (179 – 156 B.C.) to the fifth century A.D.[11] The equally important Wang Bi (A.D. 226 – 249) version, *Laozi zhu* (*zhu* means annotations), dominant since the Song dynasty, also begins with the *Dao* stanzas. These two major commentaries, by Heshang gong and by Wang Bi, were attached to *Dao De Jing* texts and were the principal vehicles for the *Dao De Jing*'s dissemination in China. There are, however, no editions of either commentary early enough to establish the original order of the two parts.

It is almost as difficult to say when *jing* became part of the title. According to a citation in the *Fayuan zhulin,* an early Tang dynasty work, *jing* (canon, or classic) was probably not added to the title of the *Laozi* until the reign of the fourth Han emperor, Jing (r. 156 – 140 B.C.).[12] This source says, with reference to the *Laozi,* simply that a *zi* (philosophical) text was elevated to *jing* (canonical) status. It does not mention the title *Dao De Jing*. In Han bibliographies the work is referred to as the *Laozi;* variants on the title *Laozi jing* also occur. The title *Dao De Jing* is said to have been spoken by the third Han emperor, Wen (r. 179 – 156 B.C.). The source is Ge Hong's

(d. A.D. 341) biography of Heshang gong in the *Shenxian zhuan*. Although probably anachronistic with respect to Emperor Wen, this quote may be the first instance of this form of the title.

Mention should be made of two important compendia of Daoist thought that contain many *Dao De Jing* passages. First is the *Wenzi,* a late Warring States (or possible early Han) text that contains lengthy essays built around formulas of the *Dao De Jing;* the essays often synthesize Confucian and Daoist terms and concepts. Second is the *Huainanzi,* a collection of essays called *xun* (teachings) that were profoundly informed by the *Dao De Jing.* These essays cover a wide variety of subjects. This work was sponsored and guided by the prince of Huainan, Liu An (179–122 B.C.).

CONFUCIUS AND LAOZI

The *Dao De Jing* is the philosophical counterpart—the rival and the complement—to the *Analects* of Confucius. These two classics are the foundational works of their respective traditions, Daoism and Confucianism, which may be said to constitute the *yin* and *yang* of Chinese culture. The *Dao De Jing* is primarily reflective in nature, while the *Analects* is more activist. Both works consist of pithy lines mixed in with longer passages, but the *Analects* is rooted in concrete historical settings and deals with specific persons and problems. In contrast, the *Dao De Jing* is without obvious historical markers and gives the impression of timeless universality. Beyond saying that these works have been traditionally associated with Confucius and Laozi, and that both works address central themes of a dramatic period of Chinese history (ca. 500–350 B.C.), there has been no scholarly consensus on how to date or even define either one.[13]

The *Dao De Jing* emphasizes the forces of nature and human interaction with them; the *Analects* emphasizes the social realm alone —human relationships, ethics, and political organization. The former stresses the relation of a transcendent *Dao* with the totality of its creation; the latter stresses hierarchical relations centering on the parent-child model and the particular obligations within clan and kingdom that are required of each person. For the former the highest authority is a maternal force that creates a gamut of ten thousand phenomena, humans but one among them; the latter honors an ancestral heaven that sanctions patriarchal dominion and elite lineage. The former idealizes the self-effacing leadership of the wise man or sage *(shengren)*, who governs himself and others by keeping to the Way; the latter idealizes the superior man *(junzi)*, a public role model who may advise the patriarch or even serve as a potential ruler in place of an unfit heir. As for religion in the sense of a deity interactive with humans, Laozi ascribes no consciousness to the Way, while Confucius, committed to an exclusive focus on human relations, cautiously advises a follower to respect the gods but keep them at a distance *(Analects* 6.20), a judicious compromise that the Chinese have by and large adhered to over the millennia.

In the West the influence of the *Analects* has been comparatively weak outside of academic circles, while the *Dao De Jing* enjoys a considerable public. It is the most popular and most frequently translated work of Chinese thought, with more than forty versions in English alone. This level of foreign interest reflects more than the text's importance in China. Its themes seem to speak aptly to the modern era, to problems that have festered for generations: economic overdevelopment and war led by those who crave power. But the work also speaks to those searching for a code of life conduct in a society where fundamental values have been degraded. For some, the *Dao De Jing* has become a cry of reason for our own war-divided world of master builders, militarists, and modernizers. For others, it is a manual for mastering one's own life by accommodating oneself not to wielded power but to nature or to force of circumstance in the broadest sense. Laozi's modern appeal may in part explain why the *Dao De Jing* has become separated from its native contexts and has perhaps been overappropriated by Western readers. And yet, as we proceed to consider its themes and historical setting, we shall see how Western apprehensions of the *Dao De Jing* have captured elements of its original significance.[14]

The Western reading public's resistance to the *Analects* may be explained by that text's emphasis on authority and discipline in its exhortations both regarding the observance of the formalities of speech, dress, and conduct, and regarding the pursuit of learning and self-cultivation for the purpose of public service. The undeniable virtues of Confucian correctness notwithstanding, there is hardly a student of Chinese culture who has not found relief in turning from the *Analects'* stern tone to the unpredictable stanzas of the *Dao De Jing* and exploring their varied themes, their ironic, almost modern, inversions, and their imaginative turns of phrase. The *Dao De Jing* presents a universal cosmic mother to replace the dead hand of paternal ancestral direction. For Laozi the social sphere is a small part of reality. Human authority accordingly is limited and must find its proper—that is, diminished—place in a far vaster context: one he calls the ten thousand things *(wanwu),* which are subject to the authority of the Way, an authority that subsumes heaven and ancestors.

CHINA IN LAOZI'S TIME

The China of the *Dao De Jing* was not the single nation we know today. There was no unified territory called China until the last twenty years of the third century B.C. Before Confucius's time, scores of small and medium-sized kingdoms were spread along the middle and eastern stretches of the Yellow and Huai river valleys. The two greatest of these kingdoms, Chu under the hegemony of Duke Zhuang and Qi under the hegemony of Duke Huan, annexed smaller kingdoms by the score and opened new land to cultivation, a process of expansion and amalgamation that continued down to the unification in 221 B.C.[15] These kingdoms of the seventh and sixth centuries B.C. recognized diplomatic and ritual obligations to a small kingdom called Zhou, situated near present-day Luoyang, which purported to be the heir of the great Zhou dynasty, founded in the mid-eleventh century B.C. The socket of the wheel, so to speak—the empty center—was the royal Zhou ruler, the son of heaven (*tianzi; tian* meaning heaven), who conferred legitimacy on regional princes, kings, and lords and their acts, including their choice of heir, but who was rarely able to impose his will on their kingdoms unless a stronger kingdom was backing him. He stood for a symbolic rather than an actual unity of the *tianxia*, the realm under heaven.

Above the son of heaven stood (or rather, walked) heaven itself, a kind of paternal oversoul whose mandate *(ming)* legitimated the rule of its "son" over the realm. Heaven comprised ancestral authority of three kinds: the immediate ancestors of the son of heaven, the founders of earlier ruling lineages, and the even more remote culture heroes (or founding fathers) of the entire civilization, such as Shen Nong, Yao, Shun, and the Yellow Emperor.

By the time of Confucius the various kingdoms had been waging many-sided wars for generations, one kingdom devouring and then absorbing another only to be itself devoured by a third power. In the period after Confucius's death in 479 B.C. new concepts and patterns of organization slowly formed and the Zhou order continued to weaken. During the decades preceding the era of Mencius (372?–289? B.C.), the philosopher who sought Confucius's mantle, the ongoing process of conquest and absorption had reduced the overall number of kingdoms, while the size and economic power of the surviving kingdoms increased. Traditionally, the era of Confucius has been called the last phase of the Spring and Autumn period, referring to the ceremonial (calendrical) authority of the royal Zhou house, while the subsequent era, the period after Confucius, has been called the Warring States period, indicating that the remaining kingdoms were increasingly independent of the Zhou son of heaven. Yet the aspiration for some unifying principle higher than the individual kingdoms remained. None of the powerful kingdoms lost sight of the goal of bringing the entire *tianxia*, the realm under heaven, under its rule. The *Dao De Jing,* some of whose stanzas speak of "capturing" the realm under heaven, has traditionally been dated to the transition from the Spring and Autumn period to the Warring States period.[16]

The period between Confucius and Mencius was a time marked by round-robin crises driven by three salient factors: serial inter-kingdom wars; accelerating economic, commercial, and technological development based on improved farming and the expansion of arable land; and political instability inside the kingdoms due to succession struggles and rising non-noble factions. These developments produced new theories of governing and state organization. Confucians, Daoists, Mohists, and Legalists—to name the principal schools—struggled to answer the problems forced into the open as the rule of Zhou weakened and the warring kingdoms grew to maturity. Initially in competition with each other, these schools increasingly tended to borrow from and even combine with one another as the process of territorial amalgamation went on and the prospect of unification loomed on the horizon.

In the philosophical competition among rival schools the *Dao De Jing* was a pivotal work of criticism and creativity. It rejected key Confucian and Mohist doctrines and at the same time opened the way for new philosophical syntheses. Penetrating and unsparing, the *Dao De Jing* transformed the terms of debate and inspired a spectrum of new ethical, political, and cosmological formulations. Its ideas could be opposed or co-opted, but they could not be ignored. To give a single example, when Laozi developed the concept of the ten thousand things, he endowed each of them with an independent identity and life momentum and freed them from any identity other than their common parentage in the Way. Guided only by their own inner momentum, the ten thousand things exist outside of the conventional network of social relationships and responsibilities, the sphere that the key Confucian terms *li*, ritual, and *yi*, obligation, roughly cover.[17] The ten thousand are not even beholden to the Way, the mother that gave them life (stanza 2), for what mother could properly attend to so vast a brood? Cast into life, any one of the ten thousand is as good as any other. There is no elite component. The indifferent Way has no career ambition for any of them. Human beings are among them, but are not preeminent. Having pursued their own natures (*ziran*, self-becoming, or what is so of itself), their seasonal cycle of life complete, they return to the Way. They do not exist to serve human ends or the developing economies of the expanding states.

The independence of the phenomena is expressed through the word *zi*, self, a term that figures in the *Analects* in only a minor way. *Zi* may be thought of as the "self" of an objective entity (see the motif word "themselves" in stanza 57). It is quite different from the Confucian term for self, *shen*, which in addition to the physical self existing in space and time also means character and social identity, thus a purely subjective kind of force to be exerted on others or on things. For Laozi, *zi* is the self as an individuated, objective other: to be viewed but not altered (stanzas 1 and 14). For the Confucians, *shen* is the self as a social instrument for molding the other in order to suit itself. In the fourth century B.C. the Confucians added the word *xing* (human nature common to all) to their lexicon to counter the concept of *wanwu* because they needed to make their concept of the self universal and objective while keeping it distinct from the more biological ten thousand things.

By making the self of all things objective and independent Laozi broke through the confining categories of Confucian thought: paternal authority, ancestor worship, and inherited privilege—categories that created a nexus of social roles and rules on which depended each person's being and consciousness. Subordinating these categories to the Way, Laozi dramatically widened the view and prepared the way for other transcendent concepts. One such concept was law *(fa)*, to which was subordinated the clan as well as the subjective judgment of its patriarch; another was receptivity or emptiness *(xu)*, which suggests open-mindedness, receptivity to differing or conflicting views. Receptivity is how the Daoists view *(guan)* the ten thousand without discrimination, with an emphasis on their collective welfare, not their usefulness to human beings. The oft-quoted summary of Laozi's thought found in the second Daoist classic, the *Zhuangzi*, says, "Gentle and yielding, modest and deferential—this was what he stood for; and with his openness and receptivity he never injured the ten thousand things—this was his actual practice." [18]

In the view of the *Dao De Jing* the wise have *ming* (insight or clarity of vision), which makes possible their appreciation of *Dao* and how it moves the ten thousand things (stanza 16). Laozi values *ming* but rejects *zhi*, a word covering intellect, knowledge, expertise, and sophistry. To Daoists *ming* is the power of the natural mind, while *zhi* refers to educated and hence artificial judgment (stanza 33). Confucians, however, value *zhi* over *ming*. In the *Analects,* *zhi* is an all-important term, *ming* an unimportant one. In the Guodian Confucian text *Wuxing* (Five categories of conduct) clarity of vision *(ming)* is a lesser faculty that leads to educated judgment *(zhi)* concerning men and affairs.

Opposed to favoritism in political practice and subjectivism in human thought, Laozi's liberating, all-inclusive vision also facilitated the development of philosophical tolerance and syncretism. In the second chapter of the *Zhuangzi* we find the concept of *qiwu*, treating all things equally by acknowledging the relativity of their qualities. Using *qi* to develop the idea of receptivity, Zhuangists advocated impartiality among diverse schools of thought, stressing the limitations of each and looking toward the accommodation of antithetical doctrines in a comprehensive argument. This same *Zhuangzi* chapter uses *ming* to denote a perspective from which opposites are reconciled and transcended. This tendency to embrace all sides became common in the philosophy of the late Warring States period (late fourth to late third centuries B.C.), as more complex governing systems promoted inclusive philosophical syntheses. Thus Laozi's critique of state development ideology paradoxically led to a higher stage of state development ideology. Put another way, the *Dao De Jing* exposed the limitations of Confucian and Mohist formulations but at the same time served as a bridge to various recombinations of the elements of Confucian, Daoist, and Legalist thought.[19] The creative application of Daoist thought to questions of law, institutional governance, and statecraft is a prominent feature of the writings collected under the names Guanzi (late fourth to early third centuries B.C.), Xunzi (mid third century B.C.), and Han Feizi (mid to late third century B.C.).

Laozi might have despaired over history's cunning, but he would have understood it. Legalism and unification were not the future he envisioned for the kingdoms of the Chinese cultural area. Perhaps the most telling revision of Laozi's thought may be the phrase "All ten thousand things take the number one as their ancestor." This formulation from the *Guanzi* chapter "Zheng" (Correct rule) reestablishes patriarchal (and masculine) authority over the ten thousand but on an abstract level and with a clear reference to law: Legalists used the number one *(yi)* to underline the idea of law's uniform application to all social strata.

CONFUCIANS, DAOISTS, AND HEREDITY

Conflict over succession was the driving force of the many-sided transgenerational civil wars of the late Spring and Autumn and the Warring States eras. Unstable inheritance patterns—who rules after the king dies?—was the critical problem that no Warring States thinker was able to master. Nearly every death of a ruler ignited a power struggle among the sons of his principal and secondary wives, and often among his brothers or even his nephews. A contender in one kingdom might seek support in a neighboring kingdom, whose intervention usually only widened the crisis. In other cases the pattern was reversed: the ruler of one kingdom, in expectation of future favors, might support a contender in a neighboring kingdom, thus instigating or intensifying the internal conflict there. The spiraling conflicts spread destruction down to the time of unification. The people of China have accepted unification (and often its counterpart, conformism) and have cherished unity ever since, in large part because of their anxiety over a divided territory and the concomitant experience of civil war. Stable central authority, when local officers answered to the center and not to the local clans, meant stable regions. But that was a China yet to come.

The Confucians recognized the seriousness of the succession problem, but they tolerated it. Hostile to law as the source of governmental authority lest it challenge the hereditary structure of noble rule itself, they strove only to convince the hereditary rulers to recruit fresh talent without consideration of birth, that is, to open family-based government to outsiders whom Confucius and his disciples were educating (precisely) for state service. They believed that an elite thus reformed and invigorated would enable the nobles to rule rightly as well as rightfully and would enable them to ensure the continuity of their rule and the attendant values of filial piety and generational continuity.

The Confucians called the new elites they were cultivating *junzi*, royal sons or true princes—men fit to succeed a king because their learning *(xue)* and virtue *(de)*, if not their birth, qualified them to serve as role models for other officials and members of society. This artificial creation of ideal noblemen to fill the many new functions in the developing kingdoms was the goal of Confucius's education program. However, Confucius was conservative, in that for him the technological and bureaucratic issues were always subordinate to the social and ethical ones.[20] He meant for his students to serve the ruler filially and to urge the ruler to treat the people as if they were his own children, avoiding war and economic disruption and educating them morally and technically. He also placed the burden of ensuring social order on the rulers, as if they were the fathers of their kingdoms.

Confucius intended to use the family as the vital core of a metafamily of *junzi* serving the new expanding state. This is why he sought to preserve filial piety and hereditary succession within the kingdoms as the keys to political order.[21] The choice of the term *junzi* for the new elite shows that Confucius was intent on remedying the problem of the defective heir and protecting the throne from the contest among the heirs to succeed the king.

The Mohists boldly veered away from the Confucians. Making an argument Socrates might have approved of, they held that ruling family interests hampered the development of the objective independent state, and so they cut the Gordian knot to separate *guo* from *jia*—state from family, kingdom from clan. One of their main slogans, "promote the worthy," was in effect a call for a ban on family preference in appointments to office. Mohists demanded that only the worthy and able should assume official position. Laozi probably knew of the Mohist critique, since he quotes the slogan in stanza 3.[22]

Both the Confucians and the Mohists were progressive state builders. Through practical and moral education they sought to develop a cadre of administrative and technical experts qualified to serve in an increasingly complex state. Laozi opposed both the Confucians and the Mohists. He looked upon economic development, new inventions, increased commerce, state building, and the recruitment of experts as destructive progress. He saw the close connection between modernization and war. He sought to return to an ancient era of content and to guide people toward a life of extreme simplicity: "Plain appearance, humble habits, / Owning little, craving less" (stanza 19). This autarkic utopia is described in some detail in stanza 80: let the kingdom be small and its people few.

Perhaps the "small kingdom stanza" affords a glimpse of the imperiled world to which Laozi belonged and in which he played an important part. According to Laozi's biography in the *Shiji*, he served in the royal court of the Zhou son of heaven as an archivist and historian. And the Zhou, itself a small kingdom—a sort of Vatican perhaps—may have been looked to by other threatened kingdoms as the last hope for protection from the aggressions of the greater kingdoms. "The greater kingdoms loathe having a son of heaven" the Han king was advised at a conference of kings in 344 B.C. "Only the smaller kingdoms benefit from it. If Your Highness and the greater powers would simply ignore King Hui [of Wei], he and the smaller kingdoms will never be able to bring back the son of heaven."[23] Laozi's biography goes on to say that he left his position as archivist because of the "decline of Zhou."

Laozi undoubtedly knew that his small utopia was unrealistic. But imagining it may have helped him to formulate other elements of his political philosophy, at the center of which is the *shengren*, a retiring sage, a wise man, who leads by staying behind, by enabling rather than visibly directing others. The emphasis on the ear in the graph for *shengren* suggests passivity: a good listener and someone to listen to as well. He receives and reacts. He is sometimes represented by the first person pronoun, *wu* or *wo,* suggesting an independent figure with no family ties except to the Way. The sage of the *Dao De Jing* has no institutional or legal context and no history. His authority is based on no lineal transmission from the past, nor can it be inherited by a future generation. Alone with the maternal Way, the sage is childlike, never a father. Whether ruler or minister (it is never clear), he undergoverns, avoids exerting influence the better to allow all to realize their inner potential, their unconditioned self-becoming *(ziran),* with no filial obligation to him or the Way. He rules a great kingdom as one cooks a small fish, hardly touching it.

Laozi's liberating vision is the reverse of paternalistic socialization based on the power of the manifest personal example of an educated elite. In *Analects* 12.19 Confucius says, "The virtue of the true prince *(junzi)* is like the wind that bends lesser men below as if they were grass." Laozi's sage is positioned below, near mother earth, not above. He seeks diversity not conformity. Child of the mother, man of the Way, the *shengren* despises "name," distinction and distinctions, and all forms of hierarchy. His powers *(de)* are within, depending on nothing external except the Way. Those he rules are his guests, not his subjects (stanza 32). He cares as much for the hopeless as for the elite (stanza 27). His self-mastery and insight win the trust of all. However, no *shengren* is ever named, no model ever cited. The *shengren* has no father or sons, genetic or spiritual. He has no ruler-vassal *(jun-chen)* relationships just as he has no father-son *(fu-zi)* relationships, the dual bond at the core of the Confucian conception of governing *(Analects* 12.11). About two centuries after Confucius's time, Mencius denounced the Daoist Yang Zhu for recognizing no ruler and Mozi for recognizing no father—two denials of authority that left humans in a state of nature, like "wild beasts" *(Mencius* 3B.9).

For Laozi the ten thousand come from the Way, not from the previous generation. Everything the Way creates returns to the Way; the Way then creates the next generation anew (stanza 14).

Subsuming all ancestry, the Way operates not in socially constructed, generational time, but in cyclical or biological time. Thus the political and cosmological aspects of the concept *Dao* converge.

TERMS OF THE *DAO DE JING: DE, DAO, TIAN*

De, conventionally translated "virtue" or "power," refers to how the Way functions (literally, walks) in the visible world. "Moral authority" is probably the closest modern English equivalent to *de*. The graph for *de* consists of three elements: walking legs on the left and on the right "mind" under "straight, go straight." Closely related to another *de* (meaning attain, obtain), *de*-virtue means the inner power to reach a result or affect a situation: charisma or dynamism, usually of a moral kind. *De* can also refer to the potency of medicinal herbs, which is also an older sense of the English word "virtue." Translators tend to prefer "virtue" as the translation for *de*; "power" is the second choice; "potency" has also been used. Generally, translators intend the original, active sense of "virtue," meaning manly, virile, derived from the Latin *vir*, and not the word's more recent, passive sense of avoiding wrongdoing or preserving feminine chastity. Perhaps it was to prevent this confusion that the translator Arthur Waley chose "power" for *de*. In the *Dao De Jing* the meaning of "virtue" depends on the meaning of *Dao*, the other half of the binary.

Dao is not a mysterious or metaphysical word. It commonly means roadway and by extension, method, and in philosophy, the path or teachings (or truths) that followers of a particular school adhere to. The *Dao De Jing* universalizes these definitions of *Dao* to the general truth that there is a course all things follow and a force that guides them on it. Laozi thus redefined and transformed the term for all time. Perhaps this was the defining moment in philosophy that divides the concepts of the Spring and Autumn era from Warring States thought, the moment when history (political and ancestral), social ethics, and personal cultivation were subordinated to a metaphysical conception framed by a pair of transcendent terms: "the Way" and "the ten thousand."

The components of the graph for *Dao*—advancing footsteps to the left of *shou* (head)—visually suggests "chief agency" or "moving first mover." Whether *Dao* is common or transcendent, something to walk upon or something higher than heaven itself—or both—is an ambiguity that informs the *Dao De Jing*. *Dao* and *de* are highlighted as a walking pair in the opening lines of stanza 21, in which *de* is described as attending or serving *(cong)* the Way—but in easy companionship *(cong-rong)*, not as master and vassal (alone, *cong* means walking behind).

For the Confucians *tian* (heaven) was more a social and patriarchal concept than a concept about nature. They understood *tian* in relation to two other terms, *de* (virtue) and *ming* (mandate). *De* and *tian* (virtue and heaven) formed the cardinal relation, a kind of religious sublimation of father and son. In the Zhou period political power was rationalized in terms of a mandate that heaven bestowed on a ruler because he had manifested virtue. The name for the construct that legitimated political power was *tianming* (heaven's mandate). These three concepts, *tian, de,* and *ming,* are central to the political thought of the texts in the Confucian canon.

Analects 2.1 says, "Government by virtue is like the polar star to whose fixed seat the multitude of stars turn in homage." In the same way the king's virtue must strive to attract and hold the mandate because, according to the ode "King Wen," heaven's mandate is not constant: it rests with the virtuous while they remain virtuous and departs when they do evil.[24] The magnetism of the ruler's virtue will draw widening circles of domains and their peoples into his orbit.

King Wen, founder of the Zhou house in the mid-eleventh century B.C., "succeeded by letting his virtue shine . . . and heaven gave its great mandate to King Wen."[25] The connection between virtue and light from the sky is often made in these writings. The ode "Shimai" says of another Zhou founder, King Wu, "May the dawning heaven above regard him as its son."[26] Throughout China's history this bond between heaven and virtue, the key to the concept of legitimacy, was in the end no more than a heightened and idealized form of the father-son relation. Confucius's "Heaven has given birth to the virtue in me" (*Analects* 7.22) moved the concept of virtue away from hereditary elitism toward a common human potentiality.

Laozi delinked virtue from a masculine heaven and reconnected it to the Way, forming a new parent-child relation and leaving heaven free to enter into new relationships—with earth, with the Way—or to remain single and independent.[27] The Chinese imagined their ancestors and culture heroes as sky walkers—planets and stars pacing the void. It was but a small step from the progenitors overhead to heaven itself as progenitor. Hence the verb "to give birth" (*sheng*) commonly follows "heaven," as it does "the Way." But Laozi's *Dao* vastly surpasses heaven in procreative capacity, bearing a full panoply of ten thousand, not just a few special heroes and ancestors. Moreover, maternal parentage is lowly, not prestigious—a reminder to all that they share humble origins with the ten thousand. As stanza 40 says, all existence comes from negation, or, in social terms, from a nonentity (*wu*).

The denial of heredity, the perpetual renewal of existence *ab ovo*, is why the *Dao De Jing* changes the unit of time measure from generation to season. History becomes nonchronological; it is an ever-present antiquity.[28] As Laozi rejects paternal guidance and heaven's authority, he also turns away from Confucian history grandly conceived as a descending procession of fathers and kings who empower the living generation with their legacy of virtue.

Hereditary time is time structured in generational tiers: Confucian time, historical time, heavenly time, calendrical time. *Dao* time is seasonal and cyclical, collapsed into the dead and the living, and so past generations cannot reach across the limit of their life spans to affect the living generations, who have unmediated access to the Way. "[T]he ghosts of the dead shall have no force" (stanza 60). Having no parent, the Way is not parental and expects no ritual offering from its offspring. They have no debt to repay to a *Dao* that did them no favor in creating them. Neither does the Way reward or punish. "Heaven and earth refuse kin-kindness: / Treating all things as dogs of straw" (stanza 5). The Way is thus a concept devised to oppose and subordinate the traditional concept of a heaven reciprocally engaged with authorized descendants or, more broadly, with human affairs.

As a graph *Dao* strikingly reconfigures the same two elements that constitute *tian* (heaven). "Heaven" is written with human legs, shortened arms, and an emphasized head. The head is represented by a flat line in modern graphs but by a circle in earlier forms. *Dao* consists of the same two elements: walking legs on the left, head on the right (not as a round skull but rather metonymically by *shou*, an eye under an eyebrow). Thus *Dao* may be thought of as a graphic synonym for heaven but in a form that somewhat conceals the anthropomorphism. The Chinese words for Great One *(taiyi)* are also a deconstruction of the graph for heaven into two sequent graphs. Another head-and-legs word, *gui* (human ghost), is represented by an enlarged head or mask over walking legs. The Way subsumes both heaven and ghosts.[29] The semantically charged graph for *Dao* has had a certain mystic power in Chinese and Japanese culture. For example, it is the *to* in *Shinto,* the Way of the Gods.

Laozi's *Dao* transcends visible heaven itself. It is unseen and unnamed—a modest, retiring female, unmarried. The virtue that accompanies it is dark *(xuan),* not shining *(ming)* like light from the sky (stanzas 10, 15, 65). Laozi challenged the basic Confucian term *mingde* (illuminating virtue) with a hidden virtue that follows the Way alone. Unlike the Confucian heaven crowded with deceased male progenitors real and mythic, the Way keeps in the background, hosts no visible bodies, no celebrities, boasts no names. As a graph, *nü,* "woman," shows a bent back and legs crossed in a half-bowing posture of service and subordination. The word for mother *(mu)* is an enlargement of the same graph. Herself invisible, inaudible, and intangible (stanza 14), she shares her graph with a form of the *wu,* what is not. In *Dao* the *yin* principle is stronger than the *yang.* Spatially *Dao* encompasses the opposites heaven and earth. Temporally it connects the categories negation and existence. The flat line, the number one *(yi),* serves as a kind of boundary between the opposites: the horizon dividing heaven and earth and also the boundary line between *wu* and *you*. The Daoists were thus creating a new philosophical language.

In every kingdom of the realm ministers, stewards, and lesser lords were overthrowing their traditional clan leaders and taking power for themselves. Usurpation from below was the order of the day. This ongoing brutal process of subversion, reorganization, invasion, annexation, and expansion characterized the world that the author of the *Dao De Jing* bore witness to and that he turned against in a prophetic manner. The New Testament sought to remake a covenant from the breakdown of the Old Testament covenant. In a comparable way the *Dao De Jing* sought to redefine philosophically and even philologically a new ultimate authority by recombining the elements, literally the pieces, of an older, ruined one.

DAO DE JING

· · · · ·

STANZA 1

1   The Way as "way" bespeaks no common lasting Way,

2   The name as "name" no common lasting name.

3   Absent is the name for sky and land's first life,

4   Present for the mother of all ten thousand things.

5   Desire ever-absent:

6   Behold the seed germs of all things;

7   Desire ever-present:

8   Behold their every finite course.

9   Forth together come the two

10 As one and the same

11 But differ in name.

12 As one, a dark recess

13 That probed recedes

14 Past that portal whence

15 The milling seed germs teem.

COMMENT   Laozi opens with a creation myth. *Dao,* a single mother, source of all life, is juxtaposed to its creation, the ten thousand things. Measured against *Dao*'s fecundity, what ancestor, what male dynastic founder, can compare? Sky and land *(tiandi)* themselves are an intermediate creation, serving the Way as a framework that imparts form and name, and thus duality, on all things as they are produced. The ten thousand move between two poles: negation and existence, unity and division, potentiality and actuality.[1] The Way describes a recurring circular or continuous S-shaped process that must return to its starting point before beginning again: "[A]ll living forms . . . go round home again" (stanza 14); "[t]he Way moves on by contra-motion" (stanza 40).

There is no human role at the level of the Way's creative power, neither for the living nor for their ancestors or the ancient god-kings. *Dao* is *chang* (everlasting, constant, common to the ten thousand): it is now as it ever has been, with no duality in itself, no historical aspect, and no ancestor or descendant. The concept of *Dao* denies paternal lineage, the foundation of hereditary privilege. The Way's ten thousand progeny—human beings among them—share a common birth mother and a common, humble, and anonymous status. They are nonentities produced of negation (stanza 40). By contrast, consider the classic Confucian formula: "Heaven gives birth to the hundred phenomena; among them humankind is noblest."[2]

Transcendent and also immanent, *Dao* resembles time or nature and is thus different from but not superior to its creation. In some contexts the Way seems indistinguishable from the ten thousand. The commentary by Heshang gong explains "common lasting Way" as nature *(ziran),* and its negation, "no common lasting way" *(fei chang Dao)* as the political rule of one era or another, that is, social constructs that time will alter. This reading is confirmed by a line in the Guodian text titled *Xing zi ming chu* (Human nature proceeds from the mandate), which says that only the "human Way" is definable.

The contemporary scholar Zhang Songru sees in this stanza a possible analogy to the atomic theories of Democritus, Epicurus, and Lucretius.[3] Laozi's imagery, however, belongs more to the realm of biology than to physics. The "seed germs" *(miao)* are fertile germ cells, not Lucretius's genderless atoms streaming slantwise through space. Nonetheless, since the antecedents of Laozi's vision are not easily found in other Chinese writings, a remote and indirect influence from the Greeks should not be absolutely excluded, especially since a possible transliteration of *ambrotos,* meaning immortal, appears in stanza 32.[4]

This stanza introduces most of the key terms that recur throughout the work: *you* (what is present, manifest, becoming; as a verb: to have), *wu* (what is absent, unmanifest, negation; as a verb: to not have), *tong* (as one, unity), *liang* (two, dual), *Dao* (Way, driving force, common path), *ming* (name, definition), *xuan* (mysterious, unseen, withdrawn, deep and dark as heaven at night, sublime; as a verb: to explore a recess), *wanwu* (*wan*, ten thousand, myriad; *wu*, figured things, *visibilium omnium*), and *chang* (common, lasting, regularly recurring, ever-present). Judging from both the text found at Mawangdui (the earliest complete text of the *Laozi* found so far) and the partial Guodian text, the term *chang* in this stanza was originally *heng*, a synonym of *chang*. *Heng* is also the name of a hexagram in the *Yijing*, or *Book of Changes*, where it stands for renewal after return to the origin, hence, circular movement.[5]

The term *tong* (one and the same) has implications often passed over, namely, that there is an underlying identity among all things arising from their common ancestry in *Dao*; furthermore, *Dao* itself is ultimately identical with its creation, thus denying the subordination of junior to senior, child to parent, creature to creator. As stanza 34 says, "The Way wins the name of humble and low." For further discussion of the relation of *Dao* to the ten thousand in terms of the tension between transcendence and immanence see stanzas 25 and 34.

In line 3 the received texts read *tiandi* (heaven and earth), translated here as "sky and land," but the Mawangdui texts have *wanwu* (the ten thousand things). "Ten thousand things" seems to resonate with the term "seed germs" *(miao)* in lines 6 and 15. The pairing of sky/land and absent/present fits the theme of emerging duality in this stanza and also in stanza 2. In line 3 the word *wu* (translated "absent") stands where "father" might have been expected. Both "absent" and "present" are female; line 3 emphasizes gestation, line 4 motherhood. *Wu* depicts a dancer with dangling ornaments, presumably female. With its faint feminine suggestion, this graph prevails in the received texts, albeit compressed and schematized. In the Guodian text the graph *wang* shows a person walking into a closed area. *Wang* with walking radical (#162) is an old form of *wu*—dance. Both negative, *wu* and *wang*, are used in modern Chinese.

STANZA 2

1 In every fair the world considers fair

2 There's foul;

3 In every good the world considers good

4 There's ill.

5 For what is what is not yields,

6 And the harder the easier consummates;

7 The long the short decides,

8 And higher lower measures;

9 Bronze gongs jade chimes join,

10 And former latter sequence form,

11 Ever round, and round again.[1]

12 This is why the man of wisdom

13 Concerns himself with under-acting

14 And applies the lesson

15 Of the word unspoken,

16 That all ten thousand may come forth

17 Without his direction,

18 Live through their lives

19 Without his possession,

20 And act of themselves

21 Unbeholden to him.[2]

22 To the work he completes

23 He lays down no claim.

24 And this has everything to do

25 With why his claim holds always true.

COMMENT   Stanza 1 sets the stage for the appearance of duality, the twins born of a prior, nameless unity. The second stanza begins with the world below *(tianxia),* where human beings create duality through knowledge and language: naming and judging, comparing and contrasting, the ten thousand. Another of the Guodian texts says, "There is human nature, there is knowledge; and then good and bad arise."[3] The opposites interact, complementing each other as much as they conflict. Note that stanza 1 is not in the Guodian text, while stanza 2 is.

Dualism as a theme may be connected with warfare. Sunzi's *Art of War (Bingfa)* names some thirty pairs of warring opposites.[4] In the chapter "Attack with Fire" ("Huogong") Sunzi writes, "Anger can be turned back to delight, and resentment to good feeling, but a fallen kingdom cannot be brought back into existence nor the dead brought back to life."

From the military strategist's narrow, purposive angle, opposition is to be exploited for an end. From Laozi's wider angle of time and nature, duality is a constant process that brings things round and round, as lines 5–11 suggest. The sage observes but does not intervene or try to exploit the process.[5]

Lines 1–2 seem to suggest that foul and fair are a twin presence, not that one resulted from or led to the other. "Forth together come the two / As one and the same / But differ in name" (stanza 1). The world of dualities is the world of forms and sounds that people sense and name, but it originates in something formless and soundless. Unlike the activist Confucian leader, who tries by his example to shape people and events within his sphere, Laozi's *shengren,* who is both a ruler and a sage, observes the interacting forms and then steps back to let events take their course and fulfill their hidden potential for reversal. The listener-sage is attentive, as the prominence of the ear in the graph for "sage" suggests. He makes no judgments, neither accepting the good and the beautiful nor rejecting the bad and the ugly. In the Mawangdui text *Cheng* (Weighing factors) speech is classified as a *yang* function, silence as a *yin* function.

Duality is the precondition for the term *wuwei,* a motif of the *Dao De Jing.* Translated as "under-acting" in line 13 of this stanza, *wuwei* in other stanzas is translated as "under-govern," "without leading," "not striving," "pursue no end." The negative *wu* (to be absent) in texts of this period sometimes interchanges with the negative imperative *wu*, which corresponds to "for" in the sense of "refrain from" in such words as "forbear," "forsake," and "forbid." Movement is implicit in the term *wei*, which means not only action and reaction but also conducting and leading forward; its earliest graph depicts a hand guiding an animal.

In the Guodian text stanza 2 follows stanza 63 and precedes stanza 32. Stanza 63 also deals with opposites. Lines 18–19 are not found in either the Guodian or the Mawangdui texts; they appear in the Wang Bi and Heshang gong texts, however. Perhaps the lines were added as a reference to stanza 1.

STANZA 3

1   Do not promote those who excel

2   And folk will have no cause to quarrel.

3   Prize not goods too hard to find

4   And people won't be turned to crime.

5   These objects of desire unviewed,

6   The people's thoughts remain subdued.

7   Thus under a wise man's rule

8   Blank are their minds

9   But full their bellies,

10   Meek their wills

11   But tough their bones.

12   He keeps the folk

13   From knowing and craving,

14   And the intellects

15   From daring to lead.

16   By acting himself without taking the lead

17   Inside his kingdom all is well ruled.

COMMENT   The slogan "promote those who excel" *(shangxian)* comes from Mozi, who urged the appointment of able commoners to government office in preference to nobles and royal kinsmen. Commoners would be rewarded for their knowledge and expertise, both technical and administrative. Laozi opposed this type of state activism *(wei)*. In his view this recruiting policy in the service of state building would only hasten the kingdoms along the path toward modernization and war, taking the common people farther and farther away from the simple life that Laozi thinks they once enjoyed.[1]

An important thinker of the generation after Confucius, Mozi broke with the Confucians and formed his own school. Opposed to Confucius's more cautious inclusion of the able among the noble, Mozi advocated an aggressive plan: to empower a new class of educated elites with high salaries and thus bind their loyalty to the ruler and give him leverage over the traditional nobles. The presence of the slogan "promote those who excel" in the *Laozi* has long been given as a reason for dating Laozi after Mozi. However, since this stanza is not found in the Guodian set of stanzas and may therefore postdate the Guodian text, its quoting of a Mozi slogan is likely.[2]

From the angle of politics and economics, Laozi opposed the policy of promoting the able because he wanted to simplify government, not develop it, and because he opposed the use of wealth— and the increased consumption it implies—as an incentive. A striking development of elite recruitment in post-Laozi Daoist political thought is found in the *Guanzi,* a syncretic text of the fourth-to-third centuries B.C. That text recommends to the rulers of Qi: "To put aside the self and establish the public good—can [the ruler] recruit the right men? To preside over state administration and appoint commoners to office—can [the ruler] place his own person last?" This passage from the chapter "Zheng" (Correct rule) shows Laozi's philosophical influence. The ruler is selfless, nonassertive, determined on strengthening the state by recruiting the able.

For Heshang gong, political order is dependent on and secondary to the ruler's personal discipline and spiritual cultivation, and his commentary on this stanza (referring to lines 1, 3, and 5) emphasizes that self-discipline: "For the sage, governing the kingdom is no different from governing the person."

The extent to which "those who excel" became an elite intellectual force is suggested by the Later Han author Wang Chong: "In the time of the six kingdoms [late fourth to mid third century B.C.] if talented ministers entered the service of Chu kingdom, its weight increased; if they departed from Qi, that kingdom's weight was reduced; if they worked for Zhao, Zhao was kept whole; if they turned against Wei, Wei suffered. . . ." So also, Mencius speaks of the renowned traveling political counselor Zhang Yi as "striking fear in the feudal lords with a single moment of rage, calming the realm when calm himself."[3] These are the "intellects" whom Laozi opposes.

In the "Jiudi" (Nine terrains) chapter of Sunzi's *Art of War* the relationship of the commander to the troops is couched in terms similar to the description of the relationship between the wise and those they govern in this stanza: "[The commander] must be able to make stupid the eyes and ears of his troops . . . driving them like a herd of sheep, back and forth, not a one knowing where he is headed."[4]

STANZA 4

1   Ever void, *Dao* provides

2   But does not fill.

3   To a welling font akin,

4   The living myriad's sacred source

5   Is like the darkness of the deep;

6   There its living presence bides.

7   Child of whom I cannot tell,

8   Liken it to the ancestor of ancestors.

COMMENT   Laozi returns to the term *Dao* and the genesis theme of stanza 1, introducing water as a metaphor for *Dao*. Often associated with the *yin* principle, water is soft, low, useful, life-giving, ever-present, common, indefinable, and vast.[1] *Dao*'s creative power is likened to a well without limit; *Dao* always remains empty because it is not subject to the oscillations (between full and empty) of duality. The source of everything, *Dao* comes from nothing; it is an orphan. Known human ancestry is limited to a succession of likenesses, a genealogy stretching back to a named clan founder. *Dao* as orphan is a prime progenitor, an ancestor more ancient and venerable than any other.[2] In it all hierarchies of historical time collapse.

    The structural problem of this stanza is whether or not to include the four triplet phrases found after line 4 in most translations. The four phrases appear in non-Guodian stanza 56, where they seem to fit in smoothly with the context of engaging the world. In the abstract and mythical context of stanza 4, however, they seem to interrupt the logic of the stanza. Gu Li excises them; Chen Guying and Gao Heng bracket them; Zhang Songru keeps them. In the present translation the four phrases are translated only in stanza 56:

"They dull their keen edge and / Resolve their differences, / Reconcile the points of view / And blend with the lowly dust."[3]

Stanza 4 is not in the Guodian text of the *Laozi*.

STANZA 5

1   Heaven and earth refuse kin-kindness:

2   Treating all things as dogs of straw.

3   Wise rulers too refuse kin-kindness:

4   Taking gentlefolk as dogs of straw.

        o   o   o

5   The space that heaven and earth frame

6   Works like a kiln-bellows and airpipes,

7   Which though emptying is not exhausted,

8   And activated, pours more forth.

9   A ruler's swiftly spent who speaks too much;

10   Better for him to guard his inner state.

COMMENT   *Ren,* "kin-kindness," is the primary value for the Confucians: it justifies the family-state as a governmental ideal. *Ren* refers to the proper affection due to the various family members but is then extended to non-family members as if they were family; hence the word is often translated as "humane" or "humanity." The biological family, however, is always the starting point. Since these first four lines are not in the Guodian text, many scholars now maintain that the criticism of *ren* is more characteristic of the non-Guodian portion of the *Laozi,* the portion closer in point of view (and perhaps in time) to certain *Zhuangzi* chapters, which are pointedly critical of Confucian values.[1]

The renowned Song dynasty scholar Su Che writes concerning the four opening lines of this stanza:

> Having no self-interest, heaven and earth encourage the ten thousand to their own self-becoming. Thus the ten thousand come into being and pass away on their own. Due to no cruelty of mine, they die of themselves; due to no kindness of mine, they come into being of themselves. They are like the sacred dog of straw, placed on the

sacrificial altar, fully adorned for the offering. Does that mean that they are cherished, or merely that their time has come? After the service they are discarded and then trampled by the departing participants. Does that mean that they are despised, or that their time has passed? The wise ruler is no different toward his people.[2]

This influential interpretation, which sees heaven as indifferent, not preferential (*ren* in the sense of humane) derives from the Heshang gong and Wang Bi commentaries. In this stanza Laozi is probably opposing Mozi's view that "heaven loves the hundred clans" (*baixing,* hundred clans) because an unjust killing will bring on a calamity from heaven.[3] Mozi's heaven cares and intervenes.

According to the *Zhuangzi:* "Before the straw dog is presented it is kept in a container that is wrapped in decorated silk. Then the personator of the dead [who receives sacrifice on behalf of the ancestral spirits] and the prayer master, after purification and abstinence, accept the container. Once the straw dog has been presented, the marchers in the ceremony trample on its head and back; the scraps and shreds of straw and grass are then collected to fire the stove."[4]

In lines 5–8, which are found in the Guodian manuscript, we find mechanical rather than biological imagery for the functions of nature. Mechanical imagery is characteristic of Mozi's thought. The Guodian manuscript passages may thus have been contemporary with or slightly later than the generation of Mozi, which was the generation following Confucius's death in 479 B.C. Joseph Needham translates *tuoyue* (translated here as "kiln-bellows and air-pipes") as "bellows and tuyere."[5]

In the *Huainanzi,* an early-Han Daoist compilation, an analogy is drawn between atmospheric phenomena and the "inner zone" of the human body; for example, the lungs are associated with *qi* (air, atmosphere). If that association was understood by Laozi, then there is a possible analogy between the *tuoyue* and the windpipe and lungs, in particular their function in speech.[6]

This macro-micro analogy, which lines 9–10 seem to point to, is the basis for the following attempt by Su Che to explain these lines:

Heaven and earth are equipped with a set of kiln-bellows and air-pipes. Once the mechanism starts moving, wherever the moving air reaches all is stirred. To the ignorant this is the acme of mechanical genius, but what do the pipes and bellows do? They remain void without collapsing. That is why they can move again and continue producing. And so ten thousand things are created, the manifold forms etched and carved between the heavens and the earth. Those who see the heavens and the earth producing fail to realize that their productivity depends on their emptiness. . . . Hence Laozi warns his reader against depleting one's spiritual potency with too much verbal expression, admonishing him to conserve the potential productive core within.[7]

There are many ways to interpret the last word of the stanza, *zhong,* a common word for inner, center, in the center or middle of, between extremes, hollow core, to hit the center of (a target). *Zhong* is also part of the title of the classic *Zhongyong,* or *Doctrine of the Mean* (in Legge's translation). Su Che takes *zhong* to mean inexhaustible inner capacity, hence in opposition to *qiong,* "spent," in line 9. This reading ties lines 9–10 (which are not in the Guodian *Laozi*), to lines 5–8. Some commentators, however, prefer to connect the closing couplet with lines 1–4 by emphasizing *zhong* in the sense of center, mean, balance of mind, equanimity—that is, indifferent in the manner of the forces of nature, which are neither kind nor cruel. Another possibility is to take *zhong* in the special sense of the empty or neutral state of the mind before it is roused to expression through emotion. This is the definition given to the word in the first chapter of *Zhongyong.* Since the textual and thematic relationship between lines 1–4 and 5–8 seems weak, lines 9–10 may have been added to connect the two quatrains through the multiple meanings of *zhong.*

In the Mawangdui text, line 9 reads: "Much fame brings frequent failures; better to preserve inner balance, empty mind."

STANZA 6

1   The valley's daemons never die,

2   The valley called the dark world womb;

3   The portal of the dark world womb

4   They call tree root of sky and land.

5   A hidden yet seeming presence,

6   Use it and stay strong.

COMMENT   The valley *(gu)* is a complex symbol. It suggests death and night as well as female; hence regeneration. According to the *Huainanzi*, "What is high governs birth; what is low governs death. Mounds and hills are male; streams and valleys female."[1]

Early dictionaries define *gu* in the sense of "valley" as a cleft in the land formed by or containing flowing water. *Gu* in this sense thus echoes the deep-water metaphor in stanza 4; it also suggests the myth of the underworld river and its daemons that nightly bring the fallen western sun back to Sunrise Valley *(Yanggu)* in the east, where after bathing in the Xian Pool, it climbs the Tree of Dawn *(Fusang)* to start the new day. Reference to the Tree of Dawn would explain "tree root of sky and land" in line 4.[2]

Some commentators connect *gu* in the sense of "valley" to *gu* in the sense of "food grains," accenting the fruitfulness of the valley. Others see the valley as a metaphor for emptiness. One scholar suggests that *gu* as "valley" refers to the lower abdomen, later called the *dantian* or "cinnabar field" of Daoist medicine.[3] This would parallel the possible analogy in stanza 5 between the space framed by heaven and earth and the chest cavity.

The Heshang gong commentary is oriented around an intuitive, subjective apprehension of the Way. This commentary's main interest is in breath and spiritual cultivation, and in this stanza it takes "dark" for heaven and "female" (translated here as "womb") for earth and then treats the nose and mouth as their counterparts: "The primal energy *(yuanqi)* of heaven enters through the nose,[4] the primal energy of earth through the mouth." Accordingly, this commentary interprets the word *gu* as a verb, "to feed spiritually," and hence line 1 to mean "nourish the spirit and it will not die."

How far to carry the apparent sexual symbolism of this stanza is an open question. According to one scholar of Chinese sexology, "Man and woman are heaven and earth; heart and genitals are fire and water; sexual arousal is the rising [*yang*] sun."[5]

Stanza 6 is not found in the Guodian texts.

STANZA 7

1 The heavens last, the earth endures.

2 And the reason why they do?

3 By disowning what they yield,

4 Heaven can last and earth endure.

5 So, surely, does the world-wise lord,

6 Who puts his interest far behind

7 And ends up in the lead,

8 Who puts his interest to the side

9 And ends up safe and whole.

10 Is it not so:

11 That having nothing to own

12 He can achieve his goal?

COMMENT   Heaven and earth disown, that is, take no personal interest in, what they create; they give life universally and impartially. The ten thousand created things *(wu)* come and go, but heaven and earth have no temporal limit. Ancestors, by contrast, produce only a single lineage but invest great interest in it, since their own limited existence is continued through subsequent generations.

An impartial, universal heaven, above and apart from the human order, was first constructed by the Mohists. They created the idea of a heaven free of ancestral domination to support a state policy that gave no preference to nobility of birth in awarding honors and offices, thus making it possible to recruit experts from the lower ranks of society. Laozi, like Mozi, seeks to separate the world of human beings and heaven but unlike Mozi tries to limit, not augment, human beings' power over nature and other humans.

Laozi's "world-wise lord" has learned the lesson of heaven and earth and refuses any self-aggrandizement through the power of his governmental position. Only in this way can a wise ruler truly serve his own interests and preserve the longevity of his life and his rule.

Stanza 7 is not found in the Guodian texts.

STANZA 8

1   Perfect mastery works like water:
2   A boon to every living creature,
3   In adverse relation never;
4   At home where most can not abide,
5   Closest to the Way it lies.
6   For position, favor lower ground;
7   For thought, profundity;
8   For engaging, gentility;
9   For speaking, credibility;
10   For ruling, authority;
11   For service, capability;
12   For action, suitability.
13   Avoiding confrontation
14   Eliminates accusation.
15   There is no other way.

COMMENT   Like heaven and earth, water has no self-interest and thus flows downward to the lowest point to serve the interests of other things without confronting or contending with them. Water "goes where others will not go, does what others will not do, in the spirit of a beast of burden, like the camel, who bears the weight and tolerates abuse."[1] This passage may be a reaction to *Analects* 19.20, in which Confucius's wealthy disciple Zi gong says, "The true prince cannot bear to be downstream where the ills and evils of the world converge." By contrast Laozi says that "He who for the kingdom's sake bears shame; / Earns the name—master of the shrine" (stanza 78). Water is adaptable but unchanging, always itself, unitary; it does not become its opposite, though it may alter all it touches. Thus water is an apt and recurring metaphor for *Dao*.

Analects 6.21 says "the wise rejoice in water." Confucius contrasts the hills, which stand for stable principles, with water, which stands for the passing flow of human activity and always remains in some relation to the hills. In the *Laozi*, however, the hills play no role; there is no duality of water and hills.

The word translated "boon" in line 2 is *li*, a primary term for the Mohists, who judge government policy by the standard of what is most useful to the people. Besides being of universal benefit, water is also a symbol of humble, even self-sacrificing, service and avoidance of conflict—two other prominent themes in the political and ethical writings of the Mozi school. Laozi has increased the beneficiaries of water to include the ten thousand things, of which people are only a minor component. Modern scholar Jiang Xichang suggests that the internal discipline Laozi calls for in stanzas 6 and 7 makes possible the mastery described in stanza 8.

Stanza 8 is not found in the Guodian texts. Nevertheless water plays a key role in *The Great Number One Gives Birth to Water,* a cosmological text that was found together with the third Guodian bundle of *Laozi* stanzas. In this text water combines with the Great One to produce heaven and earth in a long meta-genealogy. A comparable genealogy is found in stanza 42.

The word *li* also means advantage, and in this sense its presence suggests water as a military metaphor. For Sunzi, water is a model for combat, not a metaphor of humble service. In the chapter called "Weakness and Strength" in his *Art of War* we find the following: "Thus in warfare there is no unchanging array of forces, and water has an ever-changing pattern. It shows godlike mastery to be able to achieve victory by changing in response to the enemy's circumstances."

STANZA 9

1 Desist before the vessel overruns.

2 Honed too sharp no blade retains its edge.

3 Treasure-filled no room remains secure.

4 Pride in wealth and place yields retribution.

5 "Tasks complete, doers retreat":

6 Such is heaven's way.

COMMENT   The examples used in this stanza suggest an audience familiar with the problem of keeping weapons sharpened and treasuries well guarded, that is, a ruling group. Here Laozi warns against crossing the boundary between the positive and the negative. In stanza 56 he advocates dulling what is keen. This too is a form of *wuwei,* or under-acting.

Line 6 includes the words *tianzhi dao,* the *dao* of heaven. Here *tian,* heaven, is a modifying noun, as in the Confucian term *tian-ming,* mandate of heaven. The second part of the compound, *dao,* does not mean the Way in Laozi's primary sense, but rather the way something works, its modus operandi. In the *Laozi* the terms "Way" and "heaven" are usually separate.

Stanza 9 is not found in the Guodian text.

STANZA 10

1   The new-moon soul aborning holds to oneness;

2   Can you keep it from being divided?

3   To center all breath-energy, to work gently

4   Can you keep as if newborn?

5   To purify the eye within

6   Can you keep without stain?

7   To care for the people and rule the kingdom

8   Must you not master under-acting?

9   Midst ebb and flow from heaven's gates

10   Must you not play the female part?

11   For your vision to reach all quarters

12   Must you not be unknowing?

13   Through giving birth and care

14   *Dao* gives life without possessing,

15   Performs without obligating,

16   Presides without controlling:

17   Such is the meaning of "hidden power."

COMMENT   There is no consensus on the first two lines of this stanza. For a survey of the various and conflicting interpretations, see the lengthy entry in Jiao Hong's *Laozi yi*. This translator's preference is to read the first word, *zai,* in the sense of beginning or renewed; the second word, *ying,* in the sense of flickering into existence; and the third word, *po,* as the *yin*-soul or moon-soul. "New-moon soul" is the translation of *ying-po.* Among the Chinese words for soul or spirit, *po* is the soul identified with the physical self, the incarnate soul perhaps; hence it must *baoyi,* preserve its unity or oneness, to avoid *li,* division and surrender to external forces.[1]

Po refers both to the soul and to a phase of the moon.[2] As a graph, *po* consists of the word "white" *(bai)* on the left and the word "ghost" *(gui)* on the right. The ghost element emphasizes the head, and the language suggests an analogy between the emerging head of the newborn and the first glimpse of the new moon. Line 3 concerns the vitality *(qi,* breath-energy or life force) of the newborn infant, who has just crossed the line from nonexistence to existence and is thus still close to the Way, still female.³ Like the dark valley of stanza 6, the moon, the night, the womb, and the *po* all belong to the *yin* principle. After a time another soul, the cloud-soul *(hun),* will combine with the new-moon soul to form a *yin-yang* duality. All things "holding *yang,* and held by *yin*" (stanza 42).

The newborn represents the absence of both knowledge and subjective assertion. As the infant matures it can "play the female part" and thus preserve some connection to *Dao.* Discussing lines 9 and 10, Jiang Xichang writes: "*Dao* is active and it is still; what it creates is male and female. The wise man stays with what is still, not what is active; he takes a female, not a male, role. The same idea is found in stanza 28, 'Acknowledge the male, but retain the female' and also in stanza 61, 'Dam holding still has ever conquered sire.'"

This stanza is important to Heshang gong, for whom spiritual development is the foundation of statecraft. As he says in his comment to stanza 3, "The sage governs the kingdom as he governs himself." The infant represents for him a lack of division between consciousness and object, an unsocialized condition, and an indifference to the outer world. Maintaining this internal cohesion is the foundation of *rou*—the Daoist virtues of pliancy and gentleness, which underlie *wuwei* (under-action, under-reaction, disinterested action, the pursuit of no end).

The word *yi,* translated as "oneness," is discussed in the comment to stanza 14 as a symbol of heaven and of the Way. Stanza 10 is not found in the Guodian *Laozi,* and the concept of oneness is not found there either. *Yi,* however, is widely found in the *Guanzi* and the *Huangdi sijing.* For example, one of the Daoist chapters of the *Guanzi,* "Xinshu, xia" (Mental functions, part 2), says, "Only the noble man [*junzi*] who holds fast to oneness can remain unchanged in the midst of change . . . can be the lord and ruler of the ten thousand." The concepts of mental concentration and singleness are found, in addition to in the *Guanzi,* in varying forms in such Warring States texts as the *Zhuangzi* and the *Mencius.* For example, a passage in *Mencius* 2A.2 says that the mind *(xin)* or the will *(zhi)* must maintain control over breath-energy and likens breath-energy to a body of soldiers or musicians governed by a unified, unmoved mind.

The term "heaven's gates" in line 9 is understood variously. Chen Guying cites four interpretations: nose and mouth, political fortunes, the principles of nature, and the point at which human consciousness engages the outer world. Chen Guying himself offers the five senses as a variant of the first interpretation.[4] His modern Chinese version of lines 9 and 10 reads, "When the senses come into contact with the external world, can you maintain stillness?"

The last line, found verbatim in stanza 51, may be a comment that has been incorporated into the main text. "Hidden" is a translation of *xuan,* dark, and contrasts with the white of the new-moon soul. The word *de* (virtue, power) is introduced here as a term (*shiwei,* "such is the meaning of"), suggesting an explanatory note to the text rather than an integral part of it. *De*'s formal appearance as the attendant to *Dao* comes in stanza 21.

STANZA 11

1   Thirty spokes join the wheel nave

2   And make of void and form a pair,

3   And a wagon's put to use.

4   Clay is thrown to shape a vase

5   And make of void and form a pair,

6   And a vessel's put to use.

7   Door and window vent a room

8   And make of void and form a pair,

9   And a room is put to use.

10   Thus the value of what is

11   Depends for use on what is not.

COMMENT   This stanza is built around the terms *wu* (negation, what is not, void) and *you* (what is, becoming formed) in a spatial context, and like stanza 2, it illustrates the interdependence of *wu* and *you*.

Wu and *you* first appear as cosmic categories in stanza 1, where *wu* is the name for heaven and earth as yet unborn, and *you* the name for the mother of the ten thousand after their birth. In stanza 2 *wu* and *you* begin the list of opposites that define and depend on each other in the everyday world. In this stanza Laozi uses three commonplace items to make his point: one should heed the unseen, the negative aspect, of anything, for that is the secret of its usefulness. *Dao* itself is the negative as philosophical principle, the negation that precedes and follows all existence and the constant *(chang)* alternation of *wu* and *you*.

In this stanza, as in stanza 5, artisanal works serve as metaphors—a probable reference to Mozi. Mozi's key term, *li* (whatever is useful socially), which was used in stanza 8, occurs again in line 10 of this stanza.

The striking image of the void at the center of the wheel where the spokes meet may be an allusion in the opening lines of *Analects* 2.1: "Government by virtue is like the pole star to whose fixed seat the multitude of stars turn in homage." This image reappears in a bureaucratic context in the phrase "the multitude of officials converge [on the center]"; the Huainanzi commentator Gao You explains this to mean: "The officials converge on the ruler like spokes on the nave of a wheel." [1]

STANZA 12

1   The five colors cause men to not see;

2   The five tones cause them to not hear;

3   The five flavors cause them to not taste.

4   The race and the chase drive men mad,

5   And rare goods lead them astray.

6   When wise men govern this is why

7   They favor the belly, not the eye,

8   The one accept, the other deny.

COMMENT   Judging by the pursuits named in lines 1–5, this stanza is addressed to an elite, probably a ruling elite, warning them (as in stanza 3) that indulgence can ruin popular morals. Laozi is calling for discipline of the ruler's character through self-denial with regard to the prerogatives of ritual luxury.

The eye stands for appetite that cannot be satisfied. The belly, in contrast, can consume only a natural portion and thus represents limited ambition and acquisition. Laozi distinguishes between the physical eye and the spiritual eye—the eye of wisdom, the mirror within. The physical eye, the eye that looks outward, is an organ of knowing *(zhi)* through perception of forms *(wu)*. *Zhi* as a graph consists of a man with head inclined plus a mouth symbolizing speech; in Chinese, knowledge implies verbalization: to know means to name. For Laozi, naming is the basis for dominating; that is, seeing leads to knowing, naming, and then to acting *(wei)*—a sequence that enlarges the capacity to appropriate the ten thousand things. Laozi opposes the development of the capacity to dominate for two reasons: to protect the ten thousand from human depredation and to protect the ruler from destruction in his attempt to dominate the objective world.

This stanza parallels Mozi's critiques of Confucian ritual extravagance and economic excess. For Mozi's advocacy of frugality see his chapters "Against Music," "Economizing on Funerals," and "Against Confucians."[1]

In the *Jingfa,* a somewhat later text, Laozi's strictures on rulers are weakened: "Those rulers who understand the techniques of rule, pursue [the pleasures of] the hunt without bringing ruin, pursue the pleasures of consumption without dissipation."[2]

The "Jinzang" (Restricting accumulation) chapter of the *Guanzi* applies Laozi's teaching of self-restraint in a different way, combining frugality with Mozi's utilitarianism: "The enlightened king refuses a beautiful palace or declines to listen to concerts of bells and drums, not because the enjoyment is meager or because he detests music, but rather because these things ruin his administration and injure agriculture, the basic occupation."

We see in both the *Guanzi* and the *Jingfa* Laozi's strong critique of luxury being tempered by compromise. We also see a crucial shift from ritual to law as the overriding organizational principle of society. Both texts absorbed key ideas from the *Laozi* even as they applied those ideas for improving and developing government administration—a project broadly referred to as Legalism, or more precisely, the Legalism of the northeast kingdom of Qi under the Tian clan (374–250 B.C.). Legalism was the institutional and ideological path to unification; Laozi had no such purposes.

1   "At favor (as disgrace) take fright:

2   Honors to the self bring woe."

3   "Explain 'At favor (as disgrace) take fright.'"

4   "What could be more dire than favor?

5   Its gain—or loss—betokens danger.

6   Such is the meaning."

7   "Explain 'Honors to the self bring woe.'"

8   "Our selves are why we suffer harm;

9   Without them what harm would there be?

10   So to the one

11   Who honors self above the world

12   Confide its care;

13   To the one

14   Who holds the self more dear than it

15   Entrust its care."

COMMENT   The key word in this stanza is self, *shen*. For Laozi honoring self means protecting it from the world. The word *shen* has many dimensions. It refers to the physical body in time (its life span) as well as in space; it also refers to the body's social extensions: personality, roles, identity, and character. *Shen* can also refer to the living generation in relation to generations past.

For the Daoists who eschew legalism and bureaucratic service, right rule depends on the ruler's abnegation. If the ruler remains uncompromised by self-interest and self-will, he will be receptive to the Way, mediating it through his rule without impediment. Adhering to the Way alone, such a ruler has no need for law or history as models. The implication of Laozi's references to a ruler using the first person pronoun *wo* or *wu* (stanzas 37 and 57) is that his *shen* has been subordinated.

This stanza should also be read in connection with the Confucian concept of *xiushen* (self-cultivation or self-enhancement), an ongoing developmental process of learning, reflection, and moral discipline for the Confucian elite whether in or out of office. In turn, the Confucian seeks to develop the king's persona so that the king can not only recognize and attract accomplished scholars who will serve him well but also emanate virtue so that the population (and his subordinates) can be disciplined with a minimum of punitive measures.

Zhang Songru comments: "The wise ruler does not exchange his self [personal integrity] for favor or disgrace, for weal or woe. Thus this stanza extends stanza 12's theme of choosing the belly over the eye. Whoever can reject the eye can be entrusted with the world because he is able to resist external attractions, which otherwise would subvert his mind or destroy his concentration." Chen Guying offers a similar reading of this stanza.

The rejection of human law in the *Laozi* was revised in the *Huangdi sijing,* which sought to reconcile Daoist and Legalist concepts of governing. Among other consequences, this entailed a shift of focus from the integrity of the self of the ruler to his security. The closing passage of "The Great Hierarchy" ("Dafen") in the *Jingfa* says, "Whoever claims kingship over the world should undervalue his own kingdom and give due importance to recruiting men of talent. In this way his kingdom will acquire importance and his person will be secure. . . . Undervalue your self and treasure those who have the Way; then your person will be valued and your laws will function well."[1] Here the Daoist idiom of the reduced self is turned into a technique for the king to ensure mastery over a bureaucracy through legalism—the reverse of the point Laozi was making.

Lines 10–15 of this stanza are quoted in the *Zhuangzi* chapter "Zaiyou": "Thus when circumstances require a man of learning and character *(junzi)* to preside over the world below the sky *(tianxia),* his best course is minimal action *(wuwei).* A minimum of acting will enable him to keep control of his emotions, which nature has ordained. Hence [Laozi] has said: [lines 10–15]." The chapter "Zaiyou" advocates rulers who transcend the opposites, such as good and evil, reward and punishment. The term *zaiyou* is contrasted with *zhi* in the sense of govern and means to leave as is, undisturbed; to tolerate and accept. Watson translates it "Let it be, leave it alone." The second part of the term, *you* in the sense of a preserve or arboretum, has an Eden-like ring.

The *Zhuangzi* chapter "Rangwang" also sets the self against the world: "[Sage King] Yao offered the world to Xu You. Xu You refused it. Yao offered the world to Zizhou zhifu; Zizhou zhifu said, 'Do not think me unwilling, but I happen to be on my way to be treated for a chronic ailment.' Thus Zizhou zhifu, while acknowledging the importance of the world, would not endanger his health for its sake."

The Epicurean-like theme of self-preservation has been associated with the uncertain figure of Yang Zhu; Mencius named Yang Zhu as the great opponent of Mozi, who had a Stoic commitment to public service. Yang Zhu represents the epitome of self-preservation *(wei wo),* the unwillingness to sacrifice "even a hair" to save the world; Mozi represents the extreme of altruism and family-transcending, self-sacrificing love in the service of state and society. In this stanza Laozi seems to apply Yang's doctrines in his own fashion. The renowned Yuan-dynasty commentator on the *Laozi,* Wu Cheng, on the other hand, suggests influence on rather than by Yang Zhu here: he suggests that stanza 13 is "the origin of Yang Zhu's theories of self-for-self's sake."[2]

Line 8 reads literally: "The reason we are in serious danger is that we have a self." The first person pronoun *(wu* and *wo)* in this and a number of other stanzas is common in Warring States military texts, where it forms a pair with *di,* enemy. A reader of that time might have expected a phrase like "The reason we are in serious danger" to be followed by some reference to a threat. Instead, Laozi's antimilitarism extends to mean opposition to all oppositions; "self and other" is the basis of all oppositions. To remove the self from opposition protects the self. Such a self alone is capable of ruling.

Lines 1–4 of stanza 20 in the received text appear at the beginning of this stanza in the Guodian text. The word *jing*, "fright," appears as *ying* in the Guodian text with the plausible meaning of "entrap." "Both favor and disgrace are like entrapment" may be the original meaning of line 1.

STANZA 14

1   Something looked for but not seen,

2   Or listened for, not heard,

3   Or reached for, not found:

4   Call one "dim," one "faint," one "slight,"

5   Not for summons nor for challenge.

6   Combined these three make one—

7   The One, the foremost number,

8   When daylit sky and dark of night

9   Have yet to be.

10   Through this One all living forms coil forth

11   Helter-skelter—how else to name it?—

12   Only to go round home again

13   To their unbodied state:

14   Form before form,

15   Guises of the unbodied,

16   Or gleams in a dim void.

17   Who can engage them?

18   Who find the foremost?

19   Who can pursue them?

20   Who find the last?

21   Hold fast to the Way of ancient days

22   To guide us through our present world;

23   To know how things began of old

24   Is to be grounded in the Way.

COMMENT   This stanza does not occur in the Guodian text. None of the *Laozi* stanzas emphasizing a metaphysically charged number one are found in the Guodian text. However, the essay called *The Great Number One Gives Birth to Water (Taiyi sheng shui),* bundled together with the *Laozi* texts, endows the number one with cosmological powers as the origin of forms and elements.

The term *yi,* "One," a single horizontal stroke, represents the dividing line between the unmanifest and the manifest, between *Dao* and the ten thousand. On one side of the line life emerges in spontaneous profusion (*min-min,* helter-skelter). At life's end all things cross back to the unmanifest state, to negation. Things do not perpetuate themselves. Things leave no legacy, no heirs. All return to *Dao,* and *Dao* then reproduces the next generation. Of the ten thousand *Dao* creates, human beings are no more than one. The privileges of status that the elite enjoy are not passed on through chains of descent but disappear in the *Dao,* the great leveler. With the collapse of generational time into seasonal time the "Way of ancient days" becomes relevant to the "present world." Invisible, inaudible, the Way supplants historic eras and their human models.

The number one divides into two, giving birth to heaven and earth (stanza 42). "One" may also refer to the horizon at dawn, which visibly divides heaven and earth. It may represent the juncture of heaven and earth, for it is a key element in the graphs for heaven and for earth. In stanza 42 the number two (suggesting heaven and earth, or *yin* and *yang*) then multiplies into ten thousand things and their names. But trace them back to before the One, and names fail. "Names are not natural *(ziran)* but manmade; the constant Way has no name; names appear after the Way is lost. The Way is called 'Way' only as an exigency. . . . If one thing has three names, then what reality do the names have?"[1]

The connection between formlessness *(wuxing)* and oneness, clearly referring to this stanza of the *Laozi,* is stated in the "Yuan Dao xun" section of the *Huainanzi:* "One has no matching pair, so it is isolate. . . ."[2] Thus form exists only as two or more: as compounds, as *yin* and *yang,* as the harmony of parts *(he),* and so on. Annotating this stanza Wang Bi says: "One is the inception of numbering" *(shu zhi shi).*

In the Mawangdui text called *Daoyuan*, formlessness suggests transcendence of heaven and earth: "Heaven cannot mantle it [no-form], earth cannot sustain it; thus it envelops heaven and earth."

STANZA 15

1   The ancient master workers of the Way
2   Had vision to perceive the subtlest force.
3   Too deep they were to recognize,
4   And since they can't be recognized,
5   One can but strain to picture them:
6   Wary, as if wading a winter river;
7   Watchful, as if threatened from all sides;
8   Stately and restrainèd, like a guest;
9   Smooth and even, like dissolving ice;
10 Impassive, even as the spacious sea;
11 Unfettered, like a restless windstorm;
12 Rough and solid, like an unwrought bole;
13 Compact and dense, like something unrefined;
14 Wide and open-stretching, like a vale.
15 If sullied they kept calm and stayed pure;
16 If secure they moved with care and stayed alive.
17 But who can do so now?
18 Those who embrace the Way do not grow too great;
19 And thus survive and overcome defeat.

COMMENT   Early-twentieth-century scholar Jiang Xi-chang says regarding stanza 15, "The previous stanza depicts the Way as something without form, image, sound, or echo. This stanza depicts the ruler who holds to the Way as someone who has no fixed shape or name, no fixed plan of action or practical policy. This is how the Way is applied to governing the self and the kingdom."

The nature similes in this stanza suggest a ruler who is receptive, perceptive, deceptive, adaptable, and self-disciplined. Textually problematic, this stanza has been variously interpreted. For two of the uncertain lines, 15 and 16, I have relied on the Guodian text. However, the Guodian text lacks lines 10, 11, 14, and 20.[1]

Shi, "recognize," in line 3 can be read as *zhi,* marked in memory. The Mawangdui text has *zhi* in the sense of "make a record of," so the *zhi* reading is more likely than the *shi* reading. Here, then, "recognized" implies being honored publicly. Another possible reading is *zhi* in the sense of "aim to emulate," that is, they are too deep for us to aspire to. The Heshang gong commentary suggests that "ancient master workers" in line 1 refers to rulers who had taken up the Way. If so, this stanza consists of a set of warnings to the ruler about his conduct and character.

The closing lines of the Mawangdui text *Weighing Factors (Cheng)* say, "The various *yin* phenomena follow the rule of the earth; the [corresponding] qualities are to be settled and steady, correct and stable. First having mastered the mode of pliancy, one becomes adept at avoiding conflict. Such is the measure of earth and the mode of the female."[2] Judging by the partial quote in *Cheng* from lines 15 and 16, Laozi's metaphors and analogies in this stanza may belong to the *yin*/earth category; therefore the passage in stanza 15 could be understood as an elaboration of "man, / Who is bound to follow the rules of earth" (*fadi*) in stanza 25.

STANZA 16

1   By reaching utmost receptivity

2   And keeping steadfast stability,[1]

3   I, as myriads come forth in profusion,

4   Contemplate their circulation.[2]

5   All multiply in fruitful growth,

6   Then bend homeward to their root.[3]

7   This going home call equilibrium;

8   Equilibrium, returning life;

9   Returning life, call natural order;

10   To know this order, inner vision.

11   Not to know it is delusion.

12   Delusion will produce misfortune.

13   Knowing order means acceptance;

14   Acceptance, magnanimity;

15   Magnanimity, totality;

16   Totality, accord with heaven;

17   Accord with heaven, with the Way;

18   With the Way, long-lasting life;

19   The self submerged will not miscarry.

COMMENT   The penultimate line of stanza 15, "Those who embrace the Way do not grow too great," leads to the word *xu* (empty, open, receptive) in line 1 of this stanza. *Xu* suggests heaven's space; while *jing* (stable, steady, in balance) in line 2 suggests earth's solidity.[4] The "emptiness" of the mind enables it to take in the objective world without distortion. *Xu* and *jing,* clear thought and physical balance, make possible *guan,* creative contemplation, in line 4.

By using the word *xu* Laozi opened the door to a complex reinterpretation of psychology and epistemology, influencing the way Mencius, Zhuangzi, Guanzi, and Xunzi analyzed the workings and powers of the mind. But the absence of such key terms as *xin*, mind, and *xing*, nature, in the *Laozi* suggests that it predates the *Mencius* (ca. 300 B.C.) and those mid-fourth-century Guodian texts in which *xin* and *xing* are crucial philosophical categories.

For Laozi and for Xunzi, the late-third-century synthesizer of Confucian and Daoist thought, the mind is a receptor. But in the *Analects* and *Mencius* the mind is a projector, an influential force (*feng*, wind). Mencius says that when the mind is in control of the physical powers *(qi)*, they can fill the space between heaven and earth and empower the benevolent, kingly ruler to unify and govern the world *(tianxia)*. Mencius also speaks of the mind shriveling from starvation if it is not nourished by righteous conduct.

Objective receptivity sees things in large perspective: the ten thousand things moving through their unceasing transformations but always following a circuit that leads home to the beginning, the root, the mother, the womb. The closing line of this stanza finds the practitioner in the womb, ready to appear as a newborn who can focus its inferior powers and perfect its receptivity. The final word, *dai* (graphically, death and fetus), means to miscarry. Or perhaps the tomb-dweller with whom this text lay would feel safer in the womb of the earth if consoled about rebirth by the stanza's vision of nature's order.

STANZA 17

1 The best of ancient kings were in their kingdoms
  hardly known;
2 Next the patriarchs, loved and widely praised.
3 Next again those the people feared.
4 Last come those whose abuse they endured,
5 Who unworthy of trust were met with distrust.
6 What care the ancients took with every word.
7 Of tasks fulfilled and works of merit done
8 The hundred families all declared,
9 "This was no one's doing but our own."

COMMENT   This stanza is a critique of the Confucians and Mohists for fetishizing and publicly celebrating in ritual and music the sages, gods, and kings of antiquity. Laozi says that the best rulers are hardly known to the ruled: more an absence than a presence, taken for granted like heaven and earth (stanza 7). Such a ruler enables the people to claim credit for their accomplishments. The last line of the stanza is elaborated upon in the "Xingshi" chapter of the *Guanzi:* "If [the ruler] attains the Way of Heaven, his deeds seem like nature itself. . . . No one realizes that he did [*wei*] them."[1]

Line 5 suggests a passage in *Analects* 12.7, where Confucius says that sufficient food, arms, and trust are the three conditions of government, and only the last is indispensable: "If the people *(min)* have no trust, the government cannot stand."

In line 8 the term *baixing,* hundred families, is more or less equivalent to *min,* people, but "hundred families" usually has a social and cultural connotation, while "people" is used more often in an economic or military context. Any land *(di)* has people *(min),* but only a kingdom *(guo)* in the Chinese-language sphere of civilization has surname-families *(xing)*. The term here may mean the leaders of communities.

This is the first stanza to introduce the theme of historical decline—the stage-by-stage loss of an ancient world until it reaches its last days of decadence. Is this the Laozi whom Sima Qian describes as leaving his post as chief librarian of the Zhou archive in despair over the decline of Zhou? Is this stanza a forerunner of the utopian stanza 80, which is not found in the Guodian text?

The received text of this stanza is virtually identical to this stanza in the Guodian text, where it begins the third set of bamboo slips and is followed by stanza 18.

STANZA 18

1   And when the olden way of rule declined,

2   The words for love and serve came in.

3   Next came knowledge and keen thought,

4   Advent of lying, sham, and fraud.

5   When kinsmen lost their kind concord,

6   They honored child- and parent-love.

7   In dark disorder ruling houses

8   Turned to loyal devoted vassals.[1]

COMMENT   The presence of the word *gu,* "and thus," at the beginning of stanza 18 in the Guodian and Mawangdui texts, both of which are unnumbered, confirms the sequentiality of stanzas 17 and 18. It also suggests that stanzas 17 and 18 form a single stanza. In the Guodian text this single stanza is placed at the beginning of the third bundle and is thus separated from stanza 19, which was published as the first Guodian stanza.

Stanza 18 further tracks historical decline in stages, each defined by a Confucian virtue. The highest Confucian virtues, *ren* and *yi* ("love" and "serve"; conventionally, benevolence and righteousness, or kin-kindness and due service) mark the first decline; *zhi,* knowledge, marks the next; *xiao,* filial piety, the next; and *zhong,* loyalty, the last. Lines 5 – 6 say literally: "When the six primary kinship roles lost their harmony, filial and parental devotion appeared." The six roles are parent, child, elder brother, younger brother, husband, and wife.

Zhang Songru writes: "This stanza develops line 5 of the preceding stanza ('[Those] unworthy of trust were met with distrust'). Kindness, duty, lying, fraud, family dissension, filial devotion, political disorder, vassal loyalty—all develop from the rulers' original loss of virtue. In the age of natural [*ziran*] virtue men were not consciously kind and dutiful, so the values and their names did not exist. When the Way was abandoned, kindness and duty were promoted to reverse the trend; but they failed."

Gu Li says: "In the first two lines . . . the Way referred to is political, not the Way that is the foundation of the universe, the source of the ten thousand things; the Way as universal source can neither decline nor be abandoned. *Ren* and *yi* are new terms, new concepts that appeared and caused heated debate only after the Spring and Autumn era began and the way of the Western Zhou was discarded; but Laozi . . . opposed them."[2]

Since the pairing of the key Confucian terms *ren* and *yi,* as in the compound *renyi,* is first found as a motif in the *Mencius,* scholars have often argued that the *Laozi* had to postdate the *Mencius,* since the *Laozi* pairs *ren* and *yi* in this stanza and the next. However, with the unearthing of the Guodian *Laozi,* which includes this stanza, it is clear that the pairing of the terms came much earlier than the *Mencius.* (The two terms are widely used in the *Analects* but never paired.) This stanza does not critique the Confucian values so much as view them as compensation for a lost era of harmony.

STANZA 19

1   Refuse the wise, dismiss the intellects,

2   The folk will reap a hundredfold;

3   Refuse kin-kindness, dismiss due service,

4   The folk again will love as child and parent;

5   Refuse craft-skill, reject all gain,

6   No thief no robber will be found—

7   These three as text do not suffice.

8   Commandments must be put in practice:

9   Plain appearance, humble habits,

10   Owning little, craving less.

      o   o   o

11   Reject the teaching of the young

12   And thereby suffer no distress.

COMMENT   Chen Guying says, "The previous stanza describes the social ills Laozi observed. This stanza proposes measures to cure them." The measures are the rejection of wisdom and knowledge (*sheng* and *zhi*). This stanza's rejection of "craft-skill" and expertise go beyond stanza 3, which merely advocates not valuing rare goods and not upholding those who excel.[1]

The modern scholar Yang Xingshun says, "The *Laozi* opposes in its entirety the culture of the old ruling class . . . a culture that has eroded the primitive simplicity of the common people and incited their desires for 'unusual products.' Such a culture is the 'beginning of disorder.' . . . Laozi proposes a utopian philosophy to lead people to reject such a culture."[2]

The point of lines 3–4 is not immediately obvious. The reference is to the Confucians' bonding together of family and political values. Treating filial devotion as the basis and model for loyalty to political authority is the aim of *Analects* 1.2: "Are not filial and frater-nal love the basis of kin-kindness?" Mencius too treats filial love *(xiao)* as the basis of kin-kindness and fraternal love as the basis of dutiful service *(yi)*. He takes both as the foundation of social and political order, elaborating on Confucius's view that the family is the basic model for the organization of the governing leadership and for the relation of that leadership to the people. The Daoist wants to separate family values *(xiaoci,* filial and parental love) from this wider application in order to restore their original vitality.[3]

Stanza 19 was placed at the beginning of the Guodian *Laozi* by the Jingmen Museum editorial staff in their publication of the Guo-dian documents in 1998. It is not contiguous with stanzas 17 and 18. One striking difference between the Guodian and all other versions of the *Laozi* is that it does not contain the militant rejection of the Confucian virtues *ren* and *yi* ("Refuse kin-kindness, dismiss due ser-vice"). The editor of the received version might well have made the change when placing stanza 19 after stanza 18, perhaps intending to strengthen the critique of *ren* and *yi* in stanza 18 and at the same time tie the stanzas together through this repetition of *ren* and *yi*.

In Wang Bi's text, lines 11 and 12 come at the beginning of the next stanza; in the Mawangdui texts as redacted by Xu Kangsheng, lines 11 and 12 end stanza 19, and most modern scholars have placed them here. However, in the Guodian text, the displaced phrase "Reject the teaching of the young / And thereby suffer no distress" *(jue xue wu you)* comes between stanzas 48 and 20. Since stanza 48 concerns the renunciation of learning, this phrase makes a fitting coda to 48, while lines 9 and 10 seem to end this stanza well. Yin Zhenhuan regards the phrase as a small independent stanza.

STANZA 20

1   How distant from condemn consent?

2   Disgust, delight, how different?

3   He whom others fear,

4   He too has to fear.[1]

    o   o   o

5   All is beyond reach and never-ending.[2]

6   High in spirits seems the crowd,[3]

7   Like celebrants at the sacrifice,

8   Or viewers on the spring-rite stand.

9   I alone, adrift with no sign of hope,

10   Deserted and without appeal,

11   Am simple as a newborn before it smiles,

12   Dejected like someone without a home.

13   The crowd seems sunny and spirited;

14   I am sullen and low,

15   And my heart without guile.[4]

16   The crowd, so busy and eager;

17   I, drawn into myself;

18   Impassive, even as the spacious sea; unfettered, like a restless wind.[5]

19   The crowd has more than it needs;

20   I am left untended.

21   The crowd has its ways and its means;

22   I am set in my ways and despised.

23   Alone and apart from all others,

24   I honor the life-giving mother.

COMMENT   "The crowd" ("the vulgar," *su*, in some texts) probably refers to the whole royal court, since those attending the sacrifice (*tailao,* the annual triple feast of ox, pig, and sheep) would hold rank. Few rulers would welcome the unsparing political analysis and harsh advice Laozi offers in stanzas 17–19, so to find the I-persona cast out in stanza 20 as a kind of alienated dissident in his own elite world is no surprise. Such is the possible logic of the Mawangdui texts and the received *Laozi* texts. In the Guodian text, however, lines 5–24 are not found.

This stanza is often read as autobiography, but some scholars take its narrative "I" to be the man who follows the Way. Many of the lines have a personal "southern" flavor, reminiscent of the rhapsodic laments of the poet-minister Qu Yuan over his dismissal by an ill-advised king. The expressive style of this stanza contrasts with the crisp, direct admonitions of the preceding three stanzas—a style more often found in the *Book of Odes (Shijing).*[6]

Su Che comments: "The wise man equalizes other and self, unifies differences . . . yet he does not ignore the laws of his time, defy his duties, or throw reason to the winds. . . . The crowd pursues any number of things and forgets the Way. The wise turn from the ten thousand and take the Way as their sole source, like a newborn feeding on one single thing."[7]

The image of the mother as sole authority has implications for power relations in clan-ruled kingdoms, including the designation of heirs and appointment to office. The image is rectified and balanced in the Mawangdui document *Jingfa,* which restores the paternal role: "Without the [model] conduct of the father, the worth of the sons will not be realized; without the virtue of the mother, the energies of the people will not be fully utilized."[8]

This is one of the most textually uncertain stanzas, with many variant readings and suspected interpolations. Few of the principal modern editions agree exactly with one another.

STANZA 21

1   Boundless virtue all-accepting

2   Attends the Way, the Way alone.

3   Assuming form, the Way reveals

4   Shapes half-seen and then half-hid.

5   In dark half-lit, a likening;

6   In light half-dark, forms visible;

7   Hidden within, the germ of life;

8   The germ of life, no thing more real:

9   It contains a thing to trust.[1]

10 From present time to ancient day

11 These names have never been forgotten;

12 Through them we can scrutinize

13 The myriad millions' genesis.

14 How do we know of their formation?

15 Through the virtue of the Way.

COMMENT   This second "genesis" stanza, reminiscent of stanza 1, introduces the word "virtue" *(de)*. This stanza is not found in the Guodian text. The opening lines link the Way and virtue for the first time in the received text, forming one of the foundational compounds of Chinese culture, *Daode*. This term takes its place alongside other primary compounds such as *tiandi* (heaven and earth), *yinyang* (negative and positive natural forces), and *renyi* (benevolence and righteousness). *Dao* and *de* are presumably the names referred to in line 11.

Elaborating on Wang Bi's comment, Chen Guying says, "The relationship of *Dao* and *de* is as follows: *Dao,* being formless, must function through phenomena, must pass through the medium of phenomena [*wu*, things] in order to manifest its capacity. *De* [virtue, power] has the capacity [*rong,* 'all-accepting'] to manifest visibly the function of the Way."

The underlying creation metaphor in this stanza, Jiang Xichang speculates, is the kiln (see stanza 5). Jiang suggests that *rong* in line 1 should mean "shaping" rather than "accepting" and is really the *rong* that means mold when enlarged with the metal radical 167: mold or form for casting a vessel.[2] This is possible, but here *rong* is more than the capacity to hold or shape; the word implies acceptance and nurture. The Way's virtue has the capacity to contain and nurture all of its ten thousand offspring, like a dutiful spouse who attends *(cong)* her husband. *De* follows *Dao* submissively, like a wife or like a loyal vassal. Both kinds of attending are denoted by *cong,* "follow, attend."[3]

The dominant graphic element in both Dao and de (in its earliest form) is *mu,* the eye. Thus when these words are paired, there may be a visual suggestion of the sacred bronze vessels of ancient times that have stylized butterflied face masks with protuberant eyes.

STANZA 22

1   Bend to not break.[1]

2   Wrong leads to right,

3   Depletion to expansion,

4   Ruin to revival,

5   Deprivation to acquisition.

       o   o   o

6   Thus the wise hold fast to oneness,

7   Their measure for this world below;

8   They make no display and thus shed light,

9   Put forward no claim and thus set patterns,

10   Do not advance and thus succeed,

11   Do not assert and thus preside.

12   By their refusal to contend

13   The world cannot with them contend.

14   Those ancient words "Bend to not break"

15   Have pith and point

16   Truly those unbroken credit them.

       o   o   o

17   "Spare speech and let things be."[2]

COMMENT   Returning to the main theme of oppositions in the world below the sky *(tianxia),* this stanza points to embracing the One as the way for the wise man to cope consistently with the world's contradictions. The phrase "hold fast to oneness" *(baoyi)* first occurs in stanza 10, where it refers to remaining unchanged and also to having no self. One cannot rule out the possibility that lines 1–5 of this stanza constitute a stanza on their own and that the *shiyi* ("thus") of line 6 is an editorial device to join the two parts into one artificial stanza.[3]

Though the world is divided into ten thousand things, the mind of the ruler must remain undivided to avoid distraction by the world's multiple claims. Oneness is a negative power. The ten thousand may contend; the ruler must take no side and thus never contends. Wei Yuan says the phrase "hold fast to oneness" is tantamount to having no self.[4]

By contrast, the following line from the "Neiye" chapter of the *Guanzi* sees oneness as a positive source of power: "To hold fast to oneness and not let it slip will enable one to be lord and master of the ten thousand things." Here the goal of the user of oneness is mastery over nature and over the political realm. Another instance of this instrumental adaptation of Laozi's thought is found in the "Xingzheng" (Contending clans) section of the *Sixteen Canons:* "Action and stillness, which achieve timeliness, are aided by heaven and earth."

For Laozi, embracing oneness is the key to avoiding contention and disintegration. The author of "Xingzheng," on the other hand, sees both danger and gain in contention: "When heaven and earth have been set in place, even the microcosmic insects engage one against the other. Men who contend are ill-fated, and yet nothing can be accomplished without contending."[5]

These applications of Laozi's ideas, possibly dating from the mid-fourth century B.C., suggest cooperation between human beings and nature. They point the way to the grand transformation of Chinese thought achieved in the mid-third century B.C. by philosopher and historian of philosophy Xunzi, who studied Laozi closely and reversed many of his formulas, advocating the conquest of nature by humans through social organization.

This stanza is not in the Guodian text.

STANZA 23

1　The whirlwind's spent before the morning ends;

2　The storm will pass before the day is done.

3　Who made them, wind and storm? Heaven and earth.

4　If heaven itself cannot storm for long,

5　What matter, then, the storms of man?

　　　○　　　○　　　○

6　But those who attend and serve the Way

7　Correspond to the Way;

8　Those who attend and serve the power

9　Correspond to the power;

10　Those who decline to attend and serve them

11　Correspond to their decline.

12　Those who correspond to the Way

13　The Way will favor;

14　And those who correspond to its decline

15　The Way will decline to favor.

　　　○　　　○　　　○

16　"Those unworthy of trust are met with distrust."

COMMENT　　　"Attend and serve" *(cong)*, normally the language of feudal vassalage, is transferred in line 6 to the relation between humankind and *Dao*. The *jun-chen* (lord-vassal) relation has no place in the *Laozi;* even the single terms *jun* and *chen* occur rarely. A person serves *Dao* and *de*. What begins as service develops into a kind of correspondence *(tong,* the same as, be with) that supersedes the ritual upward identification of subordinate to superior.

Laozi's use of *tong* could be a critical thrust at the Mohist school. The "Shangtong" chapter of the *Mozi* gives priority to corresponding to one's social or bureaucratic superior and finally to heaven as defined by the Mohists. This stratified structure is the key to social stability for the Mohists. *Tong* also plays an important role in "Strategies," a chapter in Sunzi's *Art of War:* "The Way is what causes the people to have the same *(tong)* thoughts as their ruler and superiors; the people thus will die with their rulers as they will live with them."

In this stanza Laozi seeks a higher level of identification *(tong).* Through identification with the Way and the power, a person can endure passing storms, episodes of political tyranny, and sustain himself over the long term. The decline *(shi,* to let slip, lose) of values from *Dao* and *de* is elaborated in stanza 38. The translation of lines 6–15 is based on stanza 38, which treats the social values—*ren, yi, li* (kin-love, honor, ritual)—as a decline. In stanza 23 those who serve the lesser values decline correspondingly.

This stanza has what seem like fragments of text for its opening and closing lines. *Xi yan zi ran,* the opening line of this stanza according to some scholars, has been moved in the present translation to the end of stanza 22. If we follow Zhang Songru and keep these four words as the opening of this stanza, the phrase could mean that the wise rule with little speech (i.e., few commands) in order to allow everything to happen naturally. "Spare speech, let nature prevail" is another possible translation. The closing fragment, line 16, echoes line 5 from stanza 17. Line 16 does not end this stanza in the Mawangdui versions.

The translation of lines 12–15 follows the Mawangdui B text. This stanza is not in the Guodian text.

STANZA 24

1   How long can you stand up on your toes?

2   How far walk with stretching stride?

3   Self-display does not illumine;

4   Self-justifying sets no pattern;

5   Self-advancement won't succeed;

6   Self-assertion cannot lead.

7   In terms of *Dao,* as has been said,

8   "Like food discarded, excess actions

9   Provoke repugnance."

10   *Dao*-keepers will indeed avoid them.

COMMENT   There is little scholarly argument over the point of this homily: over-acting is self-defeating. Standing and walking are natural norms. To strive to rise above others risks security of position; to try to outpace others risks reaching the destination. All forms of self-promotion, like discarded food or unwanted action, achieve no success and earn universal disgust.

The Heshang gong commentary applies the first line to the conduct of a ruler: "Standing up on tiptoe means that those who crave power and strive for glory will not be able to establish their name or put the Way into practice for any length of time." Accordingly, this commentary takes line 10 to mean that those who keep to the Way will avoid such rulers.

Some of the lines of this stanza in the Mawangdui text differ. For example, line 1 reads: "He who blows on the stove first cannot do so standing up." This line is reflected in the late-Han *Xiang'er* text, whose first line, "Those who puff hard cannot last," sounds like a proverb or perhaps a reference to a yogic breath practice.

The *Xiang'er* (Wishing to approach) commentary says that forced breathing cannot be sustained, as it is incompatible with mental clarity and quietude.[1]

STANZA 25

1   Manifesting material in form unshaped,

2   Born before heaven and earth themselves,[1]

3   Unseen, unheard, above, apart,

4   Standing alone ever true to itself,

5   Swinging in cycles that never fail,[2]

6   Mother of heaven and earth, it seems,

7   But I know not how to give it names.

8   Pressed, I shall dub it the moving Way,

9   Or call it by name the all-supreme,

10   All-supreme and passing-beyond,

11   Passing-beyond and reaching-far,

12   Reaching-far and reverting-back.

13   Indeed the Way is all-supreme,

14   And heaven too, and earth, and man—

15   The four things in this world supreme,

16   And among them one is man,[3]

17   Who is bound to follow the rule of earth,

18   As earth must follow heaven's rule,

19   And heaven the rule of the Way itself;

20   And the moving Way is following

21   The self-momentum of all becoming.

COMMENT   Which is more valued, the mother or the child? One of the principles of priority within the ruling families with multiple wives was "the mother is honored for the child; the child for the mother."[4] This means that the mother's status depends on having a child or on the career of that child, and the child's fortunes rest with the power of its mother's family. Laozi implicitly addresses the succession question by making the female figure superior to the power of the patriarchs. After their birth the myriad children of the Way move farther away from their source until they begin their return to the mother and eventually reunite with her.

The stanza ends dramatically and unexpectedly. In lines 17–20 the levels of authority ascend from man (or king) to earth, heaven, and the Way. But in line 21 (echoing the "reverting-back" of line 12) Laozi reverses direction in a kind of transvaluation of authority, making the Way itself subject to the totality of its creation, the ten thousand.[5]

Presenting the world of becoming as the ultimate authority accents one aspect of *chang* (constant, common): the ongoing everydayness and commonplaceness of all things engaged in becoming. Compare the last lines of stanza 64: "In this way [the wise] support and sustain / The self-becoming of the myriad."

The "Shangtong" chapter of the *Mozi* suggests a similar transvaluation of authority. After describing ascending levels of political authority, Mozi argues that the son of heaven, the highest political authority, is himself answerable to a heaven that has been defined not as something higher but as something lower, as something commonplace—a "humble" heaven that simply wants all people to work for their mutual benefit. Heaven for Mozi is not remote and mysterious but accessible and obvious. Mozi likens the will of heaven to a carpenter's measuring instruments, thus locating heaven's authority in the common man.

This stanza appears in the Guodian manuscript, though it contains a few uncertain characters. It is followed by lines 5–8 of stanza 5.

STANZA 26

1   As weight anchors lightness
2   And calm governs impulse,
3   The wise leader, all day on the march,
4   Stays by his stockage train
5   Within his guarded cordon,
6   Safely positioned, beyond harm's reach.
7   Could the lord of ten thousand wagons of war
8   Risk his own self for the sake of the world?
9   Let such lightness lose him his anchoring base?
10 Such impulse his rule?

COMMENT   A military metaphor is presented for the first time. Many scholars, however, often seek to conceal or soften the military aspect of Laozi's thought. In particular, they have treated lines 3–6 in a moralistic or aesthetic manner, which, however, contradicts the remainder of the stanza. Thus in line 3 the ordinary term for an army on the march is usually interpreted as a gentleman or a sage traveling. Another part of disguising the intent of line 3 is the substitution of *shengren* (sage, wise ruler) for *junzi* (leader). The word "sage" is rarely seen in a military context; hence the change.[1]

Gu Li proposes peeling back this overlay and restoring a military reading, and his suggestion is adopted in the present translation. Gu Li regards the *Laozi* primarily as a work of statecraft. Accordingly, he connects this stanza to stanza 36, which ends: "Like fish down deep that cannot be lured / Hold craft of policy far from view." In this regard Gu Li belongs to the Han Feizi tradition of interpretation. Han Feizi, the legalist policy adviser of the late third century B.C., says of this stanza, "The stock wagons represent political power; Laozi warns the ruler never to leave his power base."

Han Feizi also says, "Power in one's own person is called 'weight' . . . which enables [the ruler] to direct his vassals."[2]

In addition to being a harbinger of stanza 30, this stanza seems thematically linked to the two that precede it: stanza 24 warns the ruler against self-assertion and stanza 25 outlines the hierarchy of authorities, while stanza 26 warns the ruler against reckless impulse. In this sense the stock wagon can be seen as a symbol of defense, in contrast to the mobile chariot used in offensive operations. The meaning of lines 5–6 can thus be recovered. They echo line 2, just as lines 3–4 echo line 1. The ruler himself is to be protected because his person is more valuable than any external temptation, even the entire realm. See also stanza 13.

This stanza is not found in the Guodian text.

1   Expert marching leaves no trails;

2   Expert wording has no flaws;

3   Expert reckoning needs no tallies.

4   Well-sealed doors have no crossbar

5   Yet cannot be opened.

6   Well-made bonds require no cord,[1]

7   Yet cannot be loosened.

    o   o   o

8   Accordingly, the wise know how to salvage men

9   And make sure none go to waste;

10   They know how to salvage things

11   And make sure none go to waste;

12   This is called far-reaching insight.[2]

13   The expert learns from the expert,

14   And draws lessons from the unfit.[3]

15   Not to value the teacher,

16   Not to hold dear his subjects

17   Is misguided in even the most learned.

18   This is called the crucial secret.

COMMENT   Commentators do not explain the connection between lines 1–7 and lines 8–16. However, lines 1–7 concern leaving something behind (or undone) that could cause trouble, and lines 8–16 warn against wasting human and material resources. Though a connection is plausible, this stanza may actually comprise two smaller stanzas.

The basic meaning of *xing,* "marching," as in an army on the march, is probably intended here, though most translations prefer "travel" or "activity." But why would a traveler want to hide his tracks? However, a column can escape detection or pursuit by covering its tracks. As in the previous stanza, a cultural aversion to militarism may have affected the reading of *xing*.

No part of this stanza is found in the Guodian text; it seems to belong with the more statecraft-oriented non-Guodian stanzas.

STANZA 28

1   Acknowledge the male,

2   But retain the female:

3   Be a drain-way for the world below the sky.

4   As a drain-way for the world below the sky,

5   Your constant power will never depart,

6   Will lead back home to infancy.

7   Acknowledge the white

8   But remember the black:

9   Be a measure for the world below the sky.

10   As a measure for the world below the sky,

11   Your constant power will never decline,

12   Will lead back home to before duality.

13   Acknowledge honors,

14   But remember humility:

15   Be a valley for the world below the sky.

16   As a valley for the world below the sky,

17   Your constant power will suffice,

18   Will lead home to stark simplicity.

      o   o   o

19   "As simplicity disintegrated useful things were forged":

20   These were the words that wise men went by

21   When serving as officers and elders,

22   For fine cutters never harm the stone.[1]

COMMENT   This stanza is about controlling the excess of a positive quality (the proud male stance) by preserving the opposite (meek female reserve). By holding to the "female" or submissive course while aware of the opposite "male" or dominant course, one can approach the unity underlying the differences and thus balance the dialectic. The low ground, the beaten track, which few contend for, leads from division and opposition back to original simplicity, harmony, and unity. The Chinese word for "drain-way" minus the water element on its left may mean "servant."

The white and black (*bai* and *hei*) of lines 7 and 8 may refer to *yin* and *yang*. Originally meaning the sunny and shady sides of a hill, *yin* and *yang* suggest day and night, and more abstractly, time. However, white and black may simply represent opposition. The closing words of line 12, *wuji,* are translated "before duality." *Ji* means the apex of a hill, where the opposing sides—sunny and shady—join. By extension *ji* means the extreme that something reaches before beginning its return. Thus the absence *(wu)* of *ji* may mean the absence of antithetical process rather than "limitless" or "infinite," as the term is often rendered.

Those in authority in a kingdom or family (officers and elders) respect the relationship between whole and part, origin and outcome, mother and child, matrix and finished form, material and product. They can "cut"—exert control, administer—without damaging the stone, that is, without severing the individuated useful item, *qi,* from its simple unwrought matrix, *pu.* The wise ruler preserves the relationship of form to origin in his administration, just as he himself remains rooted in his own origins.[2]

STANZA 29

1   Whoever mean to take this realm and rule it—

2   I see them failing to attain that end.

3   For this realm below, a sacred vessel,

4   Never may be subject to such rule.

5   They ruin it who try,

6   Lose it who hold on.

      o   o   o

7   All living things of form

8   Now move ahead, now trail behind;

9   Now breathe hot, now cold;

10   Now wax strong, now fade;

11   Now are safely set, but soon will fall.

12   And so the wise stay far from

13   All extremes, all surfeit, all grandeur.

COMMENT   The ruler who puts from himself the will to aggrandizement is as respectful of living things as he is of religious objects. He observes things in their growth and decline but makes no effort to control or exploit them. As sacred to him as the temple vessels, the ten thousand shall not be desecrated by appropriation.[1]

The term *shenqi*, "sacred object" or "sacred vessel," in the first half of the stanza is contrasted with *wu*, "living things," in the second half. One example of a sacred vessel as a symbol of political power would be the sacrificial tripod *(ding)* of the Zhou son of heaven that the messenger from Chu coveted for his king.[2]

STANZA 30

1   Those who guide their leaders by the Way

2   Will not urge war to dominate the world,

3   For such a course is bound to haunt its taker.

4   Fields where armies camp grow thorns and weeds,

5   And plague and famine follow every war.[1]

6   With the fruits of victory desist;

7   Never seek to break a beaten foe,

8   And flaunt no prowess with the victory,

9   Assert no strength, show no pride;

10   Be a victor against your will,

11   A victor who will not dominate.

12   "Beware old age in pride of manly might":

13   This warns to work not against the Way.

14   "Work against the Way, die before your day."[2]

COMMENT   Lines 6–11 suggest a code of noble restraint by the victor in war, perhaps an aristocratic ethic more proper to the Spring and Autumn period than to the Machiavellian calculations of the Warring States era. This could mean a Spring and Autumn date for this stanza, or it may simply be a reminder of a lost code of honor.

One interpretive tradition sees the *Laozi* as a book on warfare. According to Tang scholar Wang Zhen, "Every one of its eighty-one stanzas has a military consideration." And Ming scholar Wang Fuzhi says that the *Laozi* is a "teaching guide for all who write on war."

Zhang Songru disagrees. "Although this stanza concerns how to wage war, it is actually using warfare to express the philosophy of 'not taking the initiative, not holding on, hence not incurring loss.' This stanza develops the previous stanza's idea that the world is a 'sacred object, not something to take charge or hold of.' Moreover, the three lines that end this stanza are rich in generalization. Laozi is speaking of more than military matters."

Comparing the position on war taken by Mozi, Mencius, and Laozi, Zhang Songru writes: "Unlike Mozi, Laozi does not decry all offensive action; unlike Mencius, he does not call the highest punishment down on all good strategists. . . . Laozi does not oppose any and all kinds of warfare . . . but 'good strategy is win and then let live.'"[3]

STANZA 31

1   Weapons of war are omens of doom,

2   To be loathed by every living thing

3   And shunned by those who keep the Way.

4   Presiding at court the leader honors the left.

5   Resorting to war he honors the right.

6   But weapons are never the leader's choice.

7   Weapons of war are omens of doom,

8   Not to be used unless compelled.

9   Above all, with mind and heart unstirred,[1]

10   To arms give no glory:

11   For to glory in arms

12   Is to sing and rejoice in the slaughter of men.

13   And singers in praise of the slaughter of men

14   Shall not in this world gain their ends.

15   Thus the left is for deeds that are blessed,

16   The right is for deeds that bring death.

17   To the left the minor commander,

18   To the right the chief general:

19   Holding the rites to honor the dead.

20   When the slaughter is great,

21   Let the leader come forth to keen for the slain;

22   The victory won,

23   To perform solemn rites in mourning the day.

COMMENT   Laozi is said to have been a native of the kingdom of Chu, the major southern kingdom in the Warring States period. According to the *Zuozhuan* (Huan 8), it was the custom in Chu to honor the left over the right—the reverse of the custom in the northern kingdoms. Since the preference for the left over the right is confirmed in the Guodian text of this stanza, this must have been a custom of some antiquity. A comment in the *Zhongyong,* attributed to Confucius's grandson, indicates that the kingdom of Chu was thought to have been traditionally more pacific than the north. Speaking of strength, the *Zhongyong* says, "There is the strength of the northern region and that of the southern. The southerners are tolerant and flexible in disciplining others, and they refuse to take revenge on those who deny the Way. Men of culture dwell in the south. To bear arms and disdain death is the strength of the north. And strong men dwell there."[2]

This stanza may have influenced other thinkers. Mencius, who claims that he warned the king of Qi against invading Yan, seems to echo Laozi's sentiment. His phrase "Those good at waging war deserve the highest punishment" closes his manifesto against war (*Mencius* 4A.14). And *Mencius* 7B.4 says, "The man who claims to be skilled in forming the battle lines, to be skilled in the making of war, is a great criminal." The text of Sun Bin's *Art of War* also contains a warning against rejoicing in warfare.[3]

This stanza is found in the Guodian manuscript, where it begins with line 4.

STANZA 32

1   The Way continues on unnamed.[1]
2   Though in its unhewn rawness low and humble,
3   None in the realm can force it to serve.[2]
4   When lords and kings to this Way keep,
5   Ten thousand things as honored guests attend.

     ○   ○   ○

6   When heaven and earth conjoined and shed sky-mead,
7   Uncommanded the people shared it fairly.
8   But the advent of rule brought names;
9   And names meant mastering restraint.
10   To master restraint ensures survival.[3]
11   The Way's a presence in the realm of men,
12   As valley streams join rivers, then the ocean.[4]

COMMENT   In this stanza, which is found in the Guodian text, a lost era of economic equity is contrasted with present regimes of social status, administrative control, and the subordination *(chen)* of nature. "Names" means names of implements *(qi)*, natural phenomena *(wu)*, and also the social divisions *(guijian)* that mark the world of opposition and conflict. However, the Way remains attainable; indeed, it is near. From this fact rulers can draw the lesson of self-diminution. The ideal ruler does not have vassals *(chen)* whom he compels to serve, but willing guests *(bin)* whom he hosts at his table. "Sky-mead," the translation of *ganlu* (literally, sweet dew), suggests an Eden-like utopia and the harmony of the banquet. The word seems to translate the first two syllables of the Greek word *ambrosia,* meaning a divine food that confers immunity to death.

Pu, "unhewn," is another key Daoist term. To one degree or another *pu* corresponds to the English words "unformed," "stark," "raw," "elemental," "uncultured," "simple." The literal meaning is an unhewn tree trunk or stump (the primitive, natural state) that humans disturbed and then carved into *qi,* useful implements.[5] For the Confucians and the Mohists the carving of wood or stone was a metaphor for the molding and refining required for socialization. *Analects* 1.5, for example, speaks of "chipping, filing, carving, and polishing" in this context.

The term *houwang,* "lords and kings," in line 4 suggests a time at the end of the fifth century or early in the fourth century B.C., the start of the Warring States era, when the central Zhou authority was challenged by rival regional powers. The designation *hou,* lord, once a title that was Zhou's prerogative to confer, was losing prestige, causing many regional lords to rename themselves *wang,* king, to assert their equality with or independence from the Zhou house. Zhou rulers were called *wang* or *tianwang,* king by heaven's decree.[6] Southern rivals of the Zhou house (such as the kingdom of Chu) had traditionally called their rulers *wang.* The lords and kings who hold to simplicity, in Laozi's view, will host the vast world of ten thousand things, just as the lowly valley stream finds its way to the rivers and to the even lower-lying ocean of infinite capacity.

STANZA 33

1 Knowledge knows others

2 But wisdom the self.

3 Power conquers others

4 But strength the self.

5 To know contentment is wealth,

6 To act with strength resolve.[1]

7 Long as those who do not lose their place may last,

8 Timeless those who die but perish not.

COMMENT A number of Confucian passages treat the cultivation of the self as the basis for knowledge *(zhi)* of others, which is in turn necessary for holding an official position. In this stanza Laozi reverses the dynamic: the objective is knowledge and mastery of the self; knowledge and mastery of others is either secondary to or not the goal of mastery of the self.

The closing word of this stanza, *shou* (timeless, immortal) is found in *Analects* 6.21, which says that the humane *(ren)* embody fixed principles and thus transcend the span of mortal life *(shou)*. This *Analects* passage is built on the integration of knowledge and humaneness, likening the former to water and the latter to mountains. Confucius's purpose is to make the functional (knowledge) dependent on the ethical (humanity), the transitory dependent on the constant. In this stanza, by contrast, knowledge is an independent faculty.

This stanza is not found in the Guodian manuscript.

STANZA 34

1   The Way moves like the turning tide,

2   Leftward, rightward, lending its aid.

3   Ten thousand on the Way depend;

4   By it they live; the Way, never shirking,[1]

5   Attains success, fulfills its tasks,

6   Without its ever being named.

7   Under its mantle all beings thrive;

8   But ruling them not, nor desiring aught,

9   The Way wins the name of humble and low.

10   All beings bend to that home of no known master,

11   And thus the Way wins the name supreme.

12   And so may the wise achieve this themselves:

13   To shun self-supremacy all of their days

14   Is the way they achieve things supreme.

COMMENT   This stanza uses the tidal motion of water *(fan)* to express the endless reversals *(fan)* of the Way as described in stanza 40: "The Way moves on by contra-motion." The phrase for its alternating movement "leftward, rightward" *(zuoyou)* also commonly refers to the ministers assisting or guiding the ruler. Since the *Laozi* never mentions the ruler-minister *(jun-chen)* relation, the implication is that the Way, either as a model or else as mediated through the sage, will guide *(zuoyou)* the ruler through the tortuous reversals of history.

The Way never seeks to dominate its offspring. This is why the Way has a humble name. But ultimately all things return home *(gui)* to the Way, and thus its name is magnified. The Way functions parentally but rejects ancestral adulation through naming and rites of gratitude.

Of the ten thousand, mankind is one and only one. By trying to dominate, humans will violate the Way and ruin themselves. Like the Way, the wise never desire to possess, control, or use any of the ten thousand. Freed of the human logic of finding means to satisfy ends, the ten thousand thrive (*hua,* flower, develop) in their own ways. By mastering restraint a person frees the creativity of the Way and attains greatness.[2]

STANZA 35

1   Maintain all semblance of the Way supreme

2   And all the world will follow your royal lead

3   And do so without harm to each other,

4   Thus sharing in peace and calm and plenty.

        o   o   o

5   The sounds of music and the banquet scene

6   May tempt the passing traveler to pause;

7   The truths we utter here are bland and plain:

8   Look, but there is nothing for the eye;

9   Listen, there is nothing for the ear;

10   But use them and they never fail to serve.

COMMENT   This stanza has the status of an independent verse, but it can be read as a continuation of stanza 34, with its closing exhortation to achieve supremacy (*da,* greatness) by not pursuing it. In line 1 the leader is advised to image or represent *(xiang) Dao,* and that is the key to his success. The graph for "supreme" is embedded in the graph for "royal" *(wang).*

Lines 5 and 6 pick up the theme of the perils of luxury and the subversion of the senses from stanza 12, as Jiang Xichang suggests. In contrast, *Dao* exists beyond the reach of the senses, a theme from stanza 14.

This stanza appears virtually intact in the Guodian manuscript. It alludes briefly to a utopian world without conflict guided by the Way, an idea treated more fully in stanza 80. It seems to interrupt the sequence of statecraft stanzas in 33, 34, and 36.

STANZA 36

1   To what you mean to draw in, first give slack,

2   And make strong what you would weaken;

3   Raise up whom you would remove,

4   And provide when you mean to deprive.

5   That is to do the unseen, unseen.

6   For over the hard and the strong

7   The soft and the weak shall prevail.

8   Like fish down deep that cannot be lured,

9   Hold craft of policy far from view.

COMMENT   Many commentators have seen the Machiavellian side of Laozi in this stanza. Jiang Xichang, for example, says that lines 1–7 "concern the ruler's techniques for controlling his ministers" and lines 8–9 "concern his power to control them." But others, such as Gao Heng, say, "These lines speak of the Way of heaven. Though they have led some to accuse Laozi of advocating subtle maneuver, that is wrong. Laozi is warning against taking what is waxing for a permanent state, against counting on the stronger, against rejoicing in promotion, against craving to be provided for."[1]

Gu Li writes:

This stanza encompasses seeing the unseen while recognizing the obvious, observing that when something is in its positive phase it is moving toward its opposite. . . . However, this stanza undeniably includes statecraft and calculation, though there have always been those who deny that side of Laozi in an effort to protect his name. Gao Heng's view is one-sided. . . . Lines like "raise up whom you would remove" refer to governing and are clearly linked to the final line. . . .

Han Feizi absorbed from Laozi ideas about statecraft and subtle maneuver. Sima Qian understood this all too well when he combined the biographies of Laozi and Han Feizi in a single chapter; in that chapter Sima Qian wrote, "Han Feizi's severity and lack of benevolence derive from the thought of the *Dao De*."[2]

Chen Guying interprets the last line to mean "Do not put on display the armed power *(li qi)* of the state."[3] But this translation of *qi* as "weapons" may be too concrete. Another possibility is "policy." For this interpretation there is support in two usages in *Zuozhuan*. The *Zuo* under Mingong 1 winter (661 B.C.) reads: "The kingdom of Lu has not abandoned the rituals of the royal Zhou house, and Lu's rule cannot be disturbed. Be advised to concentrate on calming the uprising in Lu and befriending their rulers. Befriend those who follow ritual; rely on solidly established kingdoms; overthrow only those kingdoms that are in confusion and disorder. This is the policy *(qi)* of a king who seeks [wider] power in the realm." This advice fits well with the implication of this stanza's last four lines: the wise ruler keeps to a soft line just as the fish keeps itself safely hidden in the depths of the water. The *Zuo* under Chenggong 2 reads: "The ruler's reputation *(ming)* and policy *(qi)* can never be shared."

This stanza is not found in the Guodian text.

STANZA 37

1 The *Dao* in constant circum-motion,

2 Pursuing no end leaves nothing not done—

3 Let lords and kings to this conform

4 And all shall turn to them in trust.

5 Should then desires assert themselves,

6 We shall humble them with stark no-naming—

7 Yes, humble them with the starkness of no-naming,

8 And thus there shall be no desire;

9 And out of the repose of no-desire,

10 The world on its own will come to order.

COMMENT   This stanza ends part 1, the *Dao* section, of the poem. For the Mawangdui editor, and possibly for Han Feizi and Wang Bi as well, this was the final stanza of the entire poem, and thus a kind of summing up. The closing vision of universal order suggests the stanza's importance. The Mawangdui text differs from the Guodian text. Because of this stanza's importance, translations of the Mawangdui and Guodian versions appear for comparison in note 4.

This stanza explicitly addresses those who hold power and urges them to take a course of inaction and restraint or, in the Mawangdui version, a course of rejecting fame. Even if this course leads to success and they win the trust of many, desire—for rulers and ruled both—must be guarded against and kept at the level of stark simplicity. This is the *yumin* policy advocated in stanza 65: keep the folk unaware.

To political rulers who conform to the *Dao* by preserving simplicity (no names, no culture, no law) the ten thousand things will offer their tribute or allegiance freely (*zi*, of themselves), without royal edicts, administrators, or armies. At the core of this stanza is the phrase *zihua,* "turn to them in trust," in line 4, which imagines the ten thousand turning in trust to the ruler who observes the *Dao.* Should this bring forth new desires to possess the ten thousand, then "we," that is, those in power, will have to suppress those desires by removing names *(ming)* from things/persons *(wu).* Since law depends on names and definitions, it is clear that rule by law has no place in this vision of no naming, in which the enlightened ruling self (*wo* or *wu*) guides the kingdom.[1]

This reading follows Gu Li's view that *hua* is used in the political sense: the response of all people to the moral influence of the king. To Gu Li, *hua* stands here for the phrase *guihua,* which means give their allegiance and accept our authority, echoing the phrase *zibin* in line 5 of stanza 32: "Ten thousand things as honored guests attend." Law does not convert; it compels. Most translations render *hua* as "transform."[2]

Like many of Laozi's stanzas, this one describes a cyclical pattern: restraint by the ruler leads to everything being done and all things turning toward him. For this reason the repeated term from stanza 1, "common lasting," (*chang,* or *heng* in the Guodian and Mawangdui texts) is translated here "circum-motion"; it describes a perpetual process.[3]

The last line is different in both the Guodian and Mawangdui texts. The Guodian has: "The ten thousand will then come to order of themselves [or: will be stabilized]"; the Mawangdui: "And heaven and earth will come to right order of themselves." The received texts all say: "And the world under heaven will be stabilized."[4] The shift from *wanwu* to *tianxia,* from "ten thousand things" to "the world under heaven," may signal an editorial touch of the Jixia Academy of the kingdom of Qi (fl. last half of the fourth century B.C.). In the *Guanzi,* a representative work of the Academy, the social benefits of governmental under-action are emphasized, rather than the benefits of *wuwei* to the ten thousand.[5]

The pronoun *wo,* "we," in line 6, referring to those in control, means "our side" in Sunzi's *Art of War* chapter called "Weakness and Strength" ("Xushi"). However, the term may also be understood in contrast to *fa,* law—that is, in contrast to an impersonal rule by principles or decrees that transcend any human authority. Laozi approves rule by a *wo,* we, but criticizes *si,* self-interest. He thus tries to overcome the conflict between personal rule and personal interest by imagining a ruler who looks to the Way for his model. As early Laozi Daoism evolved into Huang-Lao Daoism in the kingdom of Qi, the Way was reconciled with the law and was even conceived of as the parent of the law.[6]

Note the phrase *shifa yongsi* (for the ruler to let go of the law and rely on himself) at the end of the "Youdu" chapter of the *Han Feizi.* This shows law and self in opposition. An almost identical phrase appears in the Mawangdui text *Cheng:* "Do not let go of law and use the self *(wo).*"

STANZA 38

1   High virtue by obliging not

2   Acquires moral force.

3   Low virtue obliges always

4   And thus lacks moral force.

5   High virtue neither strives

6   Nor acts for its own ends.[1]

7   Low virtue does not strive

8   But acts for its own ends.[2]

9   High kindness does strive

10   But not for its own ends.

11   High service also strives

12   And does so for its ends.

13   High ritual not only strives

14   But, compliance failing, stops at nothing

15   To compel conformance.[3]

16   Thus the loss of the Way

17   Meant the advent of virtue,

18   The loss of virtue

19   The advent of kindness,

20   The loss of kindness

21   The advent of service,

22   The loss of service

23   The advent of ritual rule.

24   Ritual rule turned loyal trust to deceit,

25   Leading to disorder.

26   All that has been learned adorns the Way

27   And engenders delusion.[4]

28   Hence those strong and true keep commitment,

29   Shun deceit,

30 Stay with the kernel that's real,

31 And shun flowery adornment,

32 Choosing the first, refusing the last.

COMMENT   This stanza is not found in the Guodian text, yet it is the first stanza of the oldest known full *Laozi*, the Mawangdui, which begins with the *de* or "virtue" half of the *Laozi*. Either the Mawangdui text is based on a different text tradition from the Guodian, or this stanza was later added to the Guodian collection, or it was not included in that collection; the answer is not known. With stanza 38 as the opening stanza, the emphasis of the entire work shifts from cosmology and cosmogony to history, social organization, and politics.

The first eight lines of stanza 38 elaborate on the concept of *wu-wei* (non-striving, non-action, withheld action) by evaluating types of action by whether or not they are assertive (*wei*, strive, act upon, have an effect upon); and whether or not they are calculated (done for the sake of, or for the name of, the doer).

The stanza describes social degeneration as the devolution of values—descending by stages from disinterested nonreciprocal benefit to others (lines 1–2) to favor done for favor, in sheer calculation of return—until it reaches the real object of its critique: *li*, ritual, which means to Laozi the complete externalization and hence falsification of human relations.[5] Ritual, cherished by all Confucians, entails exchange through mutual obligation: one side acts, and must act demonstratively (as in adornment) in expectation of reciprocal favor—indeed in order to oblige favor. Thus coercion is implicit in ritual.[6] The strongest refutation of this stanza's view is found in the opening chapter of the *Book of Ritual:* "The Way, virtue, benevolence, righteousness—all depend on ritual for their achievement."[7]

Unlike *li* (ritual), *de* (virtue) is an inner quality. In *Analects* 9.17, *de* is contrasted with *se* (appearance, appeal, countenance): "I have yet to find one who loves the inner quality so much as the outward show." Confucius, too, was suspicious of the tendency of ritual to mere display, but he only argued for greater frugality and simplicity in ritual. Mozi followed Confucius on this point. Laozi, on the other hand, opposes ritual in toto and never speaks of reforming it. Water exemplifies Laozi's social ideal: "Perfect mastery works like water" (stanza 8). Water performs its service in common, humble, self-sacrificing fashion; obligating no one, it is scarcely noticed and demands no thanks. This is "high virtue." "Low virtue" seeks its reward from people, from heaven, or from the ancestral gods. The chapter "Lie Yukou" in the *Zhuangzi* elaborates on some of the themes in this stanza. Compare, for example, the phrase "There is no crime greater than virtue conscious of itself" *(zei moda hu de youxin)*.

STANZA 39

1   From ancient time the foremost number

2   Has kept the heavens clear and pure,

3   The earth below firm and secure,

4   And made its spirits animate,

5   And its vales exuberant,

6   Enabled beings to procreate,

7   And kings and lords to tell their fate.[1]

8   Without that one prime integer

9   Heaven would crack, since not kept pure,

10 And earth would split, since not secure.

11 Spirits would fade, since not vital,

12 And valleys fail, since not fruitful.

13 All things would die, not procreating,

14 And kings would fall, their fate mistaking.

    o   o   o

15 The noble by the lowly are sustained;

16 Those above must have support below.

17 Hence lords and kings themselves proclaim

18 "Bereft," "bereaved," or "humble slave,"

19 Relying on a lowly name.

20 Is it not so?

21 Thus "frequent praising brings no fame."

22 "Prefer not jade's gentle chime

23 To dull stone's harsher tang."

COMMENT   Stanza 38 describes the manifestation of the
Way through virtue; stanza 39 describes the manifestation of the
Way through the number one. Stanza 38 combines the historical

and the political and ends with a critique of ritual; stanza 39, on the other hand, combines the cosmological and the political and ends with a critique of elegant music.[2]

Interpretation of this stanza depends on the definition of *yi* (one, the prime integer) given in stanza 14. In that stanza, the number one, standing between the Way and the ten thousand things, is a metaphor for the actualization of the Way in all things—a common denominator that undergoes development and complication. One is the first number but also the lowest, the beginning of the ten thousand, all of which depend on it just as the high and mighty depend on the lowly. In one crucial respect Laozi's "one" differs from later numerological formulas such as *taiyi* in the *Yijing* or in the Guodian text *Taiyi sheng shui* (The great number one gives birth to water): Laozi's "one" is always subordinate to the Way. It also differs from the use of "one" in political contexts in the *Mencius* and in Mawangdui texts other than the *Laozi*, where it refers to political unification of the kingdoms.[3]

The contrasting images of precious jade and humble stone bring the stanza to a conclusion. This kind of thematically inspirational couplet is often found at the opening of a poem in the *Book of Odes*. The Han commentator Yan Zun says, "As an object jade is fine and rare, while a rock is heavy and commonplace. Thus the former is considered noble the latter of little worth."[4] The issue of social status is underscored by comparison with *Analects*, *Mencius*, and *Xunzi* passages that use the pure tone or polished surface of jade as metaphors for the superior man *(junzi)*.[5]

The general function of "one" in this stanza is to show that *Dao* not only gives birth to the ten thousand but, as heaven and earth, has to mother and sustain them too. The horizontal line representing "one" can be seen as a metonym of the graph for "heaven" (which has a straight horizontal line on top) and an anticipation of the later term *yuan* (origin), the graph for which also has a straight horizontal line on top.[6] Another graph in this cluster is *ri*, sun, which has a straight horizontal line in the center of an oblong box (bone and bronze inscriptions, on the other hand, show a circle with a large dot in the middle). These associations between the number one, the sun, and heaven may be what endow the graph with its numinous power, a power reflected down to modern times in honorific epithets for Japanese as well as Chinese emperors.

If the flat line also represents the ground, as in graphs such as *dan,* dawn, and *li,* standing, we have to consider Yin Zhenhuan's suggestion that *yi* here refers among other things to the primacy of agriculture (the fruitful valleys).[7]

"One" plays a part in the *Guanzi* chapter titled "Neiye" (Tasks for the inner man). A passage in this chapter reads: "Who holds the one and does not lose it can be the lord of the ten thousand. When a true leader commands things and is not commanded by them, it is because he has attained the principle of the one." This passage shows the transformation of Laozi's concept of one into an active empowering principle. In the *Guanzi* chapter "Zhiguo" (Governing the kingdom) the number one is linked to the priority of agriculture in ensuring economic prosperity.

Dao and the one are also distinct in name and function. *Dao* is no more than a contrived name (stanza 25), while one is a function, a dynamic unity of two, as in stanza 42: "A duad from this monad formed. / The duad next a triad made; / The triad bred the myriad."[8]

STANZA 40

1   The Way moves on by contra-motion;

2   Yielding is the application.

     o   o   o

3   Becoming begets all beings below,

4   Becoming begotten of negation.[1]

COMMENT   In stanza 2, *you* and *wu,* a key pair of antonyms for Laozi, are translated as "what is" and "what is not." Here,
because they suggest two mutually dependent processes—a building up and a breaking down—they are translated as "becoming"
and "negation."[2]

The oft-cited lines 3 and 4 are usually rendered: the ten thousand things issue from what is *(you);* what is itself issues from what
is not *(wu).* Perhaps "nonentity" as a translation for *wu* better captures the social point: that humans share a common ancestry with
all things, an ancestry that derives from nothing and is thus no
source of pride or status, no justification of superiority and domination. The Huang-Lao legalists shifted this idea of a transcendent
factor to which all are subject from the cosmic to the social, as in
the phrase from the *Guanzi:* "Ruler and vassal, high and low, noble
and mean all comply with law."[3] In the *Guanzi,* law itself is the social application of the Way.

For Laozi the emphasis is on the social microcosm within the
natural macrocosm. No complex state machinery is envisioned. He
never uses the common phrase "ruler and vassal" *(junchen).* Classed
as one of the ten thousand, humans descend from negation and
then return to negation. In this primitivist model, the Way is best
applied by receding, by remaining no more than a part of the ten
thousand, thus yielding *(ruo,* weakness, passivity) and moving back-
ward, that is, toward negation. Compare this with the emphasis on

ruo (meaning gentleness) in stanza 78: "What more gentle in this world than water? / Yet nothing better conquers hard and strong."

The Mawangdui texts place the first half of stanza 42 directly following this stanza and place the intervening stanza 41 in front of this stanza. Yin Zhenhuan argues that lines 3–4 of stanza 40 and lines 1–8 of stanza 42 make a coherent stanza, while lines 1–2 of stanza 40 sum up the paradoxical themes of the previous stanzas.[4]

STANZA 41

1   When men of service hearken to the Way,

2   The lofty strive to see it applied,

3   The average cannot seem to decide,

4   While the lower sort grandly deride.

5   Their derision makes *Dao*'s reputation.

6   So the *Words of Guidance* says:

7   "Seers of the Way seem not to see,

8   And those who advance, to retreat.

9   The smoothest path seems unsure,[1]

10   Honored virtue seems undistinguished,

11   Ample virtue unqualified,

12   Resolute virtue undependable,

13   Stable virtue unfaithful.

14   Pure white seems impure,

15   Broad planes lack angles,

16   Great works take time,

17   Mighty voices rarely sound,

18   Grand vision has no set design,

19   Unknown the Way and thus unnamed."[2]

20   But the Way it is, the Way alone,

21   That brings first motions to fruition.[3]

COMMENT   The Way manifests itself in duality and works by contra-motion (stanza 40): what unfolds reverses what seems to be, only to be itself reversed. Thus naming is confounded. Those who see the world this way may themselves appear different from what they are; for they avoid self-display and self-assertion (stanza 24) and "Acknowledge the white / But remember the black" (stanza 28).

"Mighty voices" is the translation of *dayin* in line 17. Another possibility (though not raised by commentators) is that the reference is to the ritual court music of the ancient sage kings. *Dashao*, for example is the music of Shun, and *shao* contains the graph *yin*, meaning sound, sound of music. The sacred music of Yao was called *Dazhang;* the sacred music of Yu was called *Daxia*.[4] The implication of "Mighty voices rarely sound" or "Mighty music rarely sounds" is that it is rare for a sage to be in power. As for "grand vision" in line 18, both the Guodian and Mawangdui texts have "heaven," not "great," so the meaning may be that the patterns or pictures in the sky—the aspects of the constellations, planets, sun, and moon—have no set configuration. People's fates are controlled by the invisible Way that surrounds them, not by the visible heaven.

Line 10 follows commentators who read *gu,* valley, as *su,* undistinguished, commonplace. This reading links the line to the theme of "blending with the lowly dust," that is, becoming part of the ordinary; see stanza 56. The geometric metaphor of line 15 is interpreted by Gu Li as principle without rigidity. Alternatively, if we take *ou* (usually translated "corners") as "angles," it might mean "the square [the upright person?] has no sharp angles."[5]

The Heshang gong commentary describes the average man of line 3 as a kind of pharisee, dedicated to Confucian learning. This stanza precedes stanza 40 in the Mawangdui texts.

STANZA 42

1   The number one of the Way was born.

2   A duad from this monad formed.

3   The duad next a triad made;

4   The triad bred the myriad,

5   Each holding *yang*

6   And held by *yin,*

7   Whose powers' balanced interaction

8   Brings all ten thousand to fruition.[1]

     o   o   o

9   By the names men most of all abhor—

10   "Orphaned," "wanting," "destitute"—

11   Kings and lords make themselves known.

12   For in this world

13   Those who take less shall have more,

14   Those given more shall have less.

15   These words men have taught

16   And so shall I teach:

17   "Who live by might never do die right";

18   These my authority, my guiding light.

COMMENT   The connection between lines 1–8 and lines 9–18 may be the primacy of the lowest. As the creation rises out of the lowest number, so political authority is effective only when it positions itself beneath all subject to it (see stanzas 39 and 61). The term *yi,* "one," is developed in "Chengfa" (Established law): "One rapidly unfolds; by the few know the many."[2]

For more on the place of the number one in the cosmological structure, see the comment to stanza 14. "Duad" may or may not refer to *yin* and *yang*—terms that occur only in this stanza; "duad" could also refer to *you* and *wu* (what is and what is not) or to *tian* and *di* (heaven and earth). The word *san* (three, triad) is a homophone of the word for disperse, disintegrate, so line 4 may be a variation on "As simplicity disintegrated useful things were forged" (stanza 28). After "three" *(san)* the formative structure expands out *(san)* to the ten thousand. Alternatively, *san* may stand for *can*, conjoin.

Lines 5 and 6 say literally "embracing *yang* and bearing *yin* on its back." These two terms are used for the interdependent opposites with which all things are endowed. Each has its respective *qi,* its powers, energy fields, or animating forces—positive and negative. For Laozi *yin* and *yang* seem to be equal and, like heaven and earth, subordinate functions of *Dao*.

Yin and *yang* became dominant concepts in the philosophical schools of the eastern Qi kingdom when the understanding of them as natural, equal forces interacting in a balanced manner was revised and they were each assigned to sets of social factors. For example, in the *Cheng* section of the *Huangdi sijing, yang* is associated with heaven, large kingdoms, sovereigns, males, and so on, while *yin* is associated with earth, small kingdoms, vassals, females, and so on. Comparable passages are found in the *Wenzi.* In this way *yang* became associated with dominance and dynamism, *yin* with submissiveness and quietism. Laozi, if anything, favored *yin* functions. In *Zhuangzi's* "Tiandao" chapter *yang* is linked to activity and *yin* to stillness, but they remain equals, as they are presented in this stanza.

Line 10 gives three humbling terms by which rulers referred to themselves. The third, *bugu* (literally, no foodgrain) may have influenced the Japanese *boku,* your servant—a common word for "I, myself." The second part of the stanza develops some of the themes of stanza 39.

STANZA 43

1   In this world below the sky

2   The gentle will outdo the strong,

3   And the nonmaterial are able

4   To enter the impregnable.

5   Thus I know and know for sure

6   The gains that under-acting yields.

7   But teaching by the word unspoken

8   In this world few can master;

9   The gains that under-acting yields

10   In this world few realize.

COMMENT   In the *Laozi* the word *rou*, translated here as "gentle," refers to water, a metaphor for *Dao*. "What more gentle in this world than water? / Yet nothing better conquers hard and strong" (stanza 78). Water is also the purposeless benefactor of the world (stanza 8). The word *rou* is familiar in English as the first syllable *(ju)* of the Japanese word *judo; do* is the Japanese reading for *dao.* Both the terms *rou* and *shui* (water) are used in military contexts, for example, in the *Sunzi,* to describe how the weak can cope with the strong.

The "Buer" (Contra diversity) chapter of the *Lüshi chunqiu* says, "Lao Dan valued *rou.*" *Rou* is thus more than a military metaphor. Its range of meaning includes flexibility, docility, gentleness—characteristics of things first forming, at the inception of their life, when they are malleable and adaptable. One opposite is *jian,* strong, meaning hard and fast, hardened into fixed form, like things at the end of their life. These antonyms are found in stanza 76, which describes the human being as soft and tender at birth but rigid and stiff at death, and plants as pliant and delicate when coming forth but dry and frail when dying.

The present stanza links the concept of *rou* (in the combined sense of docile and emergent) with the concept of *wu* ("nonmaterial," or "nonexistent," in line 3). This link suggests that the nonexistent includes the potential—something that does not yet exist but is in process of formation. *Wuwei* ("under-acting" in line 6), then, suggests an action that is fluid, attuned to the emerging possibilities of a situation.

In stanza 28 the word *ru*, humility—related phonetically to *rou*—is the key virtue to be preserved. In stanza 78, the idea of enduring disgrace is linked to kingly conduct: "He who for the kingdom's sake bears shame / Earns the name—master of the shrine." Thus the concept of *rou* can be further extended to include "bearing shame."

Rou is a necessary tactic for the government of a weaker, smaller kingdom that has to cope with powerful ambitious neighbors. This suggests not a small kingdom that is merely trying to survive, but one that has a *tianxia*, a "realm-wide" perspective from the center—a kingdom like that of the royal Zhou house itself. This recurring view from the center is important for positioning the *Dao De Jing* philosophically and chronologically, since disdain for the realm and its problems is the hallmark of certain post-Laozi Daoists, notably Zhuangzi, who is noted for his refusal to serve in office, and Yang Zhu, who advocated a self-protecting, self-valuing philosophy and opposed any bid for political power.

For a revision of Laozi's formulation, see the "Sanjin" section of the *Huangdi sijing* text *Jingfa:* "The Way of men includes both soft and hard; the soft [alone] cannot be used, the hard [alone] cannot be relied upon."[1]

Another word in the *rou* family is *ruo* (weakness, yielding). As stanza 40 says, the Way works through weakness and in this manner controls the myriad phenomena—a cosmic expression of the power of the gentle over the strong. Thus the terms for weakness and yielding are used in the *Laozi* on both the social and the cosmic levels.

The Heshang gong commentary says, "The nonmaterial *(wu)* means the *Dao,* which has neither shape nor substance yet moves in and out of what seems solid and impenetrable to reach the spiritual. . . ." "Nonmaterial" may also refer to consciousness, or to something spiritual that can enter into and even transform something physical. The subtle working of the nonmaterial can alter the internal dynamic of the material and thus prove more effective than overt declarations or direct action.

STANZA 44

1   Is the name or the man the more precious?
2   Does the man or his goods count for more?
3   Does the gain or the loss bring more pain?
4   Extreme economies entail great waste,
5   And excess holdings heavy losses;
6   But a humbling is spared by few wants,
7   A miscarriage by knowing the limits;
8   Thus one can abide and endure.

COMMENT   *Ming,* "name," includes honor, face, fame, title, and rank, as well as personal terms of address—all of which register social status and function.[1] Whether social order is sustained by ritual or by law, name is the instrument for its common acceptance and enforcement. Names also serve to describe the realm of the ten thousand, and when so used become a device by which people through social organization appropriate the ten thousand for their own consumption.

Despite their major differences, Laozi and Mozi shared a conservative outlook on economics, based on a preference for limited productivity. Mozi had criticized funerary ritual for its extravagance and had singled out the wastefulness of "music," that is, great entertainment festivals. By the early to mid third century B.C. there was a sea change in the sphere of economics. In the writings of Xunzi, who borrowed heavily from Laozi but for purposes opposite to Laozi's, one finds a sense of burgeoning productive power, making the self-limiting economics of Mozi and Laozi seem obsolete. For Xunzi the human economy is not antagonistic to nature but rather creatively integrates itself with nature, drawing upon it for expansion and improving nature in the process. The final object of Xunzi's philosophy is the conquest of the ten thousand things, a conquest that envisions their use for human beings rather than their own independent (zi) self-development. Laozi would probably have grieved at Xunzi's application of his philosophy of minimizing human impact on nature.[2]

STANZA 45

1   Great successes may seem flawed,

2   But their benefits injure no one.

3   Great abundance may seem spent,

4   But its supply is endless.

5   Great honesty may seem unfair,

6   Great eloquence like reticence,

7   Great artistry like clumsiness,

8   But they stand the trial of use.

9   Keen cold yields to excitation,

10   And heat of passions to repose:

11   On reflection and repose rely

12   To rightly rule the world below the sky.

COMMENT   Hovering over this stanza is a sense of military dialectics. Sun Bin's chapter "Ten Questions" ("Shiwen") in *Art of War* says that when attacking a strong and large army, "Announce your lack of courage; display your lack of ability; passive and clumsy, await the foe, in order to make them arrogant and weaken their determination; thus the enemy will not know [what you are doing]."[1]

The word *qing*, translated here as "reflection," is usually translated as an adjective (pure, limpid) but is almost surely a noun in this stanza, equal syntactically to "repose." *Qing* means clear water, or clear as water, but it also means made clear by refining (as in wine). Applied to conduct, the word means clean; applied to thought, it means clear, suggesting concentration, or refining reflection. Both understanding, which extracts the vital essence of things, and repose, which is the power to resist temptations, are required for the ruler to see the negative and positive sides of things. Lines 9 and 10 may simply be folk aphorisms concerning the interaction of contraries.[2] Reflection and repose are Laozi's method for dealing with the relationship between contraries. As Wang Bi says in his comment to this stanza, "Through reflection and repose [wise men] attain the various 'greatnesses' mentioned earlier."

Building on Wang Bi's comment, Su Che writes:

> Honesty without flexibility is honesty that must break; honesty must follow the inner law governing things, and even if it twists and turns, it is honesty. Art without crudeness is art that will lose its appeal; but if art stays close to things as they are, though crude, it is art. Eloquence that leaves nothing unsaid is eloquence that will exhaust itself; but speech that conforms to principles, though reticent, will be eloquent.
>
> Unflawed success, unfailing bounty, inflexible honesty, facile artistry, loquacious eloquence—these are all like energy that cannot find repose, or repose that cannot be aroused. For activity can overcome cold, but cannot overcome heat; repose can overcome heat, but cannot overcome cold. Each is trapped in its one-sidedness and thus is not objective. Only dispassionate reflection and repose are immune to onesidedness.[3]

STANZA 46

1   When the Way prevails below the sky
2   Disbanded chargers dung the land;
3   But when the Way the world deserts
4   War horses breed outside the towns.

o   o   o

5   No crime exceeds desire sanctioned,[1]
6   No woe is worse than discontent,
7   No omen more dire than desire gained.
8   Truly with few wants content,
9   Contentment lasts as long as life.

COMMENT   The first four lines of this stanza are not found in the Guodian text. The complete stanza form is in the Mawangdui text, with the first four lines set off in the A text. Apparently, the Mawangdui editor wanted to link the antiwar theme with the theme of controlling desire. Thus the desires of the ruler—ambitious expansion and acquisition—become the focus of the stanza. But in fact desire is a broad category of which military ambition is only a subsection.

The most common interpretation of line 4 is that meeting increasing demand for horses requires bringing female horses into field camp and battleground—once good farmland—to breed. *Jiao* (suburb, countryside) is contrasted to the administrative center in the *Book of Odes*. The Heshang gong commentary says that the female horses give birth in the war camps because the war has kept them from returning home for so long.

STANZA 47

1   No need to venture past the door

2   To know this world below the skies,

3   Nor peer outside the window frame

4   To see the heavens' works and ways:

5   "Distant ventures, meager knowledge."

6   For this reason men of wisdom

7   Know the world not having walked it,

8   And name it true not having seen it,[1]

9   And gain success not striving for it.

COMMENT   The world of Laozi was filled with educated elite who traveled widely as diplomats. Their mission was to arrange alliances and treaties, both military and commercial. These *youshui,* circulating persuaders, were renowned for their knowledge of history and current events and for their skill in talking rulers and advisers into staying a course or changing one. Another category of travelers was the scholars who flocked from many kingdoms to the Jixia Academy in the kingdom of Qi.

In this stanza Laozi opposes the "open door" epistemology of broad engagement with the world of objects and forms. He shuts out the outside world and severs intercourse with it in order to maintain clarity about it. For example, "Interdict all interaction; / Seal and bar all gates and doors" is the formulation of stanza 52. Laozi's claustrophilia echoes his accent on the female, who was confined to domestic spaces and had no place in public.[2]

The image of a secure interior from which to view more clearly the outer world profoundly affected the eastern, or Qi, branch of Daoist Legalism. This school is represented in the *Huangdi sijing* and in the *Guanzi,* whose chapter "Mental Functions" ("Xinshu, shang") says: "Cleanse the palace and throw wide its portals. The palace refers to the mind, and the mind is the place where understanding dwells. The gates refers to the senses, the means to see and hear."[3] Though the architecture in the *Guanzi* passage has changed from the humble abode implied in this stanza of the *Laozi,* the epistemology is consistent: knowledge is a function of internal discipline and cultivation. For Laozi, however, the mind is the primary resident of its abode; for the author of the *Guanzi* chapter, clear consciousness is a kind of guest (*guiren,* treasured person) who may not enter if the lodgings are not to his liking or may depart if the service is inadequate.[4] Mental clarity is essential for the proper control and utilization of the senses. When desires are suppressed, the mind controls its officers, the senses. The *Guanzi* passage thus amends Laozi's rejection of the senses (stanza 12), claiming instead that purity of mind is the precondition for the successful acquisition of objective knowledge through the senses.

In later texts such as the *Han Feizi* and the *Huainanzi* this stanza was used to support the idea that the sovereign could never know enough to govern by his unaided powers; he had to rely on the knowledge that was brought to him by others.

STANZA 48

1   To pursue learning, learn more day by day;

2   To pursue the Way, unlearn it day by day:

3   Unlearn and then unlearn again

4   Until there is nothing to pursue:

5   No end pursued, no end ungained.

       ○   ○   ○

6   Whoever means to win this world below

7   Never undertakes that task;

8   Whoever does make that his task

9   Is not fit to win this world below.[1]

COMMENT   Learning *(xue)* means striving to know the world beyond the door, the world that Laozi dismisses. The purpose of learning was expansion and extension, the acquiring of ever-wider bureaucratic, diplomatic, and technical expertise. Laozi opposes such learning because it leads to economic development, territorial expansion, and war. This is the theme of lines 1–5.

In the Guodian text, line 6 is the orphaned line that opens stanza 20 in the received text, but which modern editors have sometimes shifted to the end of stanza 19: *jue xue wu you,* "Reject the teaching of the young / And thereby suffer no distress." This four-word line (two lines in English) probably completes the present stanza as found in the Guodian manuscript. Note also the connection between this stanza and stanza 38 made in the *Zhuangzi* chapter "Zhibeiyou" (see notes to stanza 38). The famous line 5 of this stanza: *wuwei er wubuwei,* usually translated "By inaction nothing is left undone," could also be translated in the potential: "Not acting makes all action possible." The line is effaced in Mawangdui A and incomplete in Mawangdui B.

Lines 6 through 9 use two military terms, *qu* and *shi*. *Qu* (win, prevail) is common in military texts, where it is used in the sense of seize or take power. Its use here in an antimilitary context is probably an intentional reversal of convention, as if to say, "This is how to 'conquer' the world." The term *shi* (task, a cause to serve) also frequently appears in military texts in the sense of military matters or factors.

Lines 6–9, which are missing in the Guodian text, were not originally a sequel to lines 1–5 but rather an independent stanza or comment added to the text to illustrate its usefulness to those in power. This fortifies the theory of Guo Qi that the Guodian text is a version of the *Laozi* that argues for return to simplicity, while the Mawangdui and all other *Laozi* texts apply that argument to the ends of statecraft.[2]

1   The wise maintain no constant mind,

2   But take as theirs the people's mind.[1]

3   "Those minded to do good we take for good,

4   As we do those not so minded":

5   And this obligates their goodness.

6   "And the trusted I trust,

7   As I trust the not-to-trust":

8   And this obligates their trust.

9   In the world the wise man stands

10   All-enfolding, all-accepting—

11   No longer apart from the world, nor above.

12   The people lend him their eyes and their ears;

13   The wise man cradles them like babes.[2]

COMMENT   The opening image reverses the conventional Confucian position on the authority of the ruler over the ruled. The Confucian ruler is the judge of right and wrong and those he rules will follow the direction he sets, as grass bends to the wind's course.

The Guodian text *Ziyi* (Dark robes) attributes to Confucius these words: "The people take the ruler to be their mind, the ruler takes the people as his body. What the mind enjoys the body feels comfortable with; what the ruler enjoys the people will desire."[3] Making the ruler and the mind the determinative factors and the people and the body the responsive factors is a commonplace of Warring States Confucian thought. In the Guodian text *Dexing* (Virtuous conduct) the mind is spoken of as the ruler of the physical senses, the people as the physical being of the ruler. Laozi's ruler does not act as a superior director, however. Like water that seeks the lowest level and yet holds sway, the mind of Laozi's ruler follows the contours of those he rules.[4]

The wise ruler is a nonjudgmental, self-effacing mother. The phrase *xi-xi*, "all-enfolding, all-accepting," in line 10 is associated with the female. Laozi's ruler does not judge, just as the mother abandons no child; this universal embrace echoes the lines of stanza 27: "Accordingly, the wise know how to salvage men / And make sure none go to waste; / They know how to salvage things / And make sure none go to waste." The closing line has the word *hai*, child (in the received version), which suggests the child in his or her mother's arms, as opposed to *zi*, the socially recognized child.[5]

With virtually no changes in text, a rather different reading of these lines is found in the Heshang gong commentary. Lines 3–4 are understood to mean that when the people do good the sage accordingly treats them as good, and when they are not good he converts them to good. The same for the trust in lines 6–7. Lines 9–10 are taken to mean that in the world the wise are anxious lest their good fortune lead to pride and profligacy. So also, lines 11–13 are interpreted: the sage allows his mind to be confused for the people's sake and so their eyes and ears have to serve him. The sage raises them with love, expecting no reward or return.

This stanza is not found in the Guodian manuscript.

STANZA 50

1   They come forth into life and they go to the dead:

2   The gateways of life are thirteen in all,

3   And the gateways of death the same thirteen.

4   But people in pursuit of life

5   Drive themselves to where death waits

6   At any of the thirteen mortal points.

7   And why is this?

8   A way of life too rich.

9   Men say those who secret themselves well[1]

10 Will meet no gaur or tiger on the land,

11 Nor suffer weapon's wound in war:

12 Present the gaur no place to gore them,

13 Nor the tiger place to claw them,

14 Nor the foe a place to stab them.

15 And why is this so?

16 Their mortal points are not exposed.

COMMENT   In "Jie Lao" Han Feizi lists thirteen vital functions: eyes, ears, nostrils, mouth, excretory organs, and the four limbs. This stanza's second half seems to speak of a kind of supernatural invulnerability not consistent with the rest of the *Laozi*. Perhaps some contact with a medical or military text led to this stanza's incorporation into the *Laozi*.[2]

A similar but more developed passage in the *Zhuangzi* speaks of the quasi-magical effects of spiritual training:

> The perfect man can walk under water without choking, can tread on fire without being burned, and can travel above the ten thousand things without being frightened. . . . This is because he guards the pure breath—it has nothing to do with wisdom, skill, determina-

tion, or courage. . . . His spirit has no flaw, so how can things enter and get at him?

When a drunken man falls from a carriage, though the carriage may be going very fast, he won't be killed. He has joints and bones the same as other men, yet he is not injured as they would be because his spirit is whole. . . . If he can keep himself whole like this by means of wine, how much more can he keep himself whole by means of heaven! The sage secrets *(cang)* himself in Heaven—hence there is nothing that can do him harm.[3]

This stanza is not in the Guodian text.

STANZA 51

1   Ten thousand *Dao* begets and breeds,

2   Which its power tends and feeds

3   As objects all take varied shape,

4   As things to use reach final form.

5   For this the natural myriad

6   Honor the Way, esteem its power.

7   Such honor and such high esteem

8   No mandate from above decreed;

9   It is their norm of self-becoming.

      o   o   o

10   *Dao* indeed begets and breeds,

11   All its power tends and feeds

12   And fosters and then raises up

13   And brings to full maturity

14   And still preserves and still protects.

15   For *Dao* begets but does not keep,

16   Works its way but does not bind:

17   Authority that does not rule.

18   Such is the meaning of "hidden power."[1]

COMMENT   In this stanza the procreative powers of the Way are cast in a parental metaphor rather than a numerological one as in stanza 42. The parental aspect of *Dao* and *de* in this stanza is reinforced by the stanza's affinities with ode 202, "Liaowo," whose fourth stanza has lines that virtually match lines 1–6 of this stanza:

> Father, he begat us, and mother, she embraced us
> And stroked us and tended us
> And fostered us and raised us

And watched us and protected us
And gave us comfort wherever she went.
To requite such virtue and favor *(de)*
Would be like requiting the heavens infinite.

This is the second and last time in the text that the terms in its title, *Dao* and *de*, are found in conjunction. In stanza 21, *de* (power, favor) is a handmaiden to *Dao*, a partner assisting *Dao*'s creative mission. The largess of *Dao* and *de* is not without design. Thus *Dao* and *de* work unseen and never look for repayment from the things they have given life to. *Dao* does not begrudge its effort; *de* does not seek repayment for gifting the ten thousand with self-becoming. This is what sublime favor or power means: it goes unacknowledged; there is no way to reciprocate. For that favor, *Dao* and *de* enjoy the honor and esteem of all things, but given freely, not in ritualized response to ordained authority. Indeed, they preempt the honor and esteem normally demanded of children and subjects.

STANZA 52

1   The world below has its gestation;

2   We hold there's a mother of all below.

3   The mother gained

4   The children known;

5   The children known,

6   The mother regained;

7   Then your life will not miscarry.

       o   o   o

8   Interdict all interaction;

9   Seal and bar all gates and doors;

10   Thus prevent debility.

11   Open paths of interaction;

12   Busy furthering your ends;

13   Then never make recovery.

       o   o   o

14   True vision marks the smallest signs;

15   Real strength keeps to the gentler way.

16   Apply your view,

17   But regain true vision's inner home.

18   Fall not into life's misfortunes;

19   Strive for the common lasting norm.

COMMENT   The first thirteen lines of this stanza combine the theme of stanza 47—"No need to venture past the door / To know this world below the skies"—with the maternal aspect of the Way. The innumerable offspring—the effects—must be "known" and kept in perspective. But the original cause should never be forgotten. Hold fast to the source of things; then the relation of *Dao* to things, cause to effect, "mother" to "child" will always be clear. As Wang Bi's comment says, "Do not neglect the fundamental and pursue the trivial." This is "true vision" *(ming)*; this is reaching "the timeless constant norm."

The second part of the stanza is a reprise of the theme of keeping the people from knowledge. Following Heshang gong, the word *dui*, "interaction," is usually taken to mean the eyes (or by extension, the senses), which receive the outside world; the gates and doors are the mouth, and perhaps hearing as well. These lines may also refer to wider commercial and political intercourse. In the *Huainanzi*, sealing in is related to *yin*, opening out to *yang*.[1]

The theme, in the third part of the stanza, of noting the smallest signs was opposed by Mencius in his description of a man with vision *(ming)* keen enough to detect a fine hair but blind to a wagonload of wood (*Mencius* 1A7.10). Interestingly, Mencius uses this analogy to advocate taking action *(wei)* to further fundamental principles and goals. Mencius saw Daoist inaction as a kind of small-scale hedonism that serves the self alone and avoids extending oneself to serve others. Mencian altruism advocates the patriarchal family as the model for the state. This is Mencius's application of his basic principle of *ren* (benevolence, humanity, kin-kindness).[2]

STANZA 53

1   Grant me this: to firmly know

2   That in walking the great high Way

3   I shall fear only to deviate

4   From the high way plain and fair;

5   For to byways men are lightly drawn.

6   The court is richly blessed,[1]

7   But the farm fields are wasting,

8   And the bins bare of grain;

9   And courtiers dress in elegance,

10   Bear well-honed swords,

11   Gorge on food and drink—

12   This superflux of wealth and goods

13   Is the piper's tune for thieves,

14   The negation of the Way.

COMMENT   This is one of the stanzas that define the *Dao* in a political context; it is not found in the Guodian text. For the most part, these protest stanzas are spread across both halves of the received text, but they tend to be more common in the non-Guodian part of the text. The criticism of abusive official power compares in its sharpness to that found in the "Rifling Trunks" and "Robber Zhi" chapters of the *Zhuangzi*. "He who steals a belt buckle pays with his life; he who steals a state gets to be a feudal lord—and we all know that benevolence and righteousness are to be found at the gates of the feudal lords."[2] In the *Zhuangzi* chapter "The Way of Heaven," Laozi, in an imagined conversation with Confucius, contrasts benevolence and righteousness *(renyi)* with simplicity *(pu)*. Notably, however, such direct attacks on *renyi*, a core Confucian term, are not found in the Guodian text.

STANZA 54

1 Virtue well-founded nothing uproots;
2 Virtue fast-bound no one can steal;
3 And this ensures through generations
4 The sacred services be not cut off.
5 Cultivated in his character,
6 His virtue pure and simple.
7 Cultivated in his clan,
8 His virtue well suffices.
9 Cultivated in his district,
10 His virtue offers leadership.
11 Cultivated in his kingdom,
12 His virtue brings prosperity.
13 Cultivated in this realm below,
14 His virtue knows no limitation.
15 This is the reason to consider
16 Character in terms of character,
17 Clan in terms of clan,
18 District in terms of district,
19 Kingdom in terms of kingdom,
20 And the world below as the world below.
21 How do I know this is true of the realm?
22 By this very means.

COMMENT Possibly referring to lines 16–21 of this stanza, a passage in the *Guanzi* reads: "You will be unable to govern the township if you treat it as a clan; you will be unable to govern the kingdom if you treat it as a township; you will be unable to govern the world if you treat it as a kingdom."[1] The *Guanzi*, in its institutional orientation, drops the issue of virtue in rule and confines itself to opposing the Confucian extension of the standards of the smaller unit to the larger—the family as the model for the state. This stanza retains the term "virtue" as the foundation for guaranteeing the continuity of the clan rites, that is, the survival of the kingdom, but it is virtue as defined in the *Laozi*.

The locus classicus for the Confucian expansion model is found in *The Great Learning (Daxue)*: self-cultivation is required for ordering the clan, ordering the clan for governing the kingdom, governing the kingdom for bringing peace to the world. Laozi proposes instead that each level of social organization be distinguished, seen, and ruled in its own terms. Confusion of the levels is caused by the aggrandizing of a lower level upon a higher. Virtue may be necessary at each level, but those of "well-founded" virtue will have the qualities requisite for that particular level. Another formulation of the same problem is found in the *Huangdi sijing* text "Liufen": "To consider the kingdom, consider the ruler; to consider the family, consider the father."

This stanza is found in its entirety in the Guodian text, where it follows stanza 45.

STANZA 55

1   Who holds within the fullest power

2   To a newborn may compare,

3   Which no insect stings,

4   No wild beast seizes,

5   No taloned bird snatches.

6   Though soft-boned and weak-limbed, its grip is firm.

7   Before it ever knows of intercourse,

8   Its standing phallus shows its full life force.[1]

9   It cries all day without a loss of voice,[2]

10 A sign of its perfect balance.

11 Knowing balance means constant norm;[3]

12 Knowing the norm means inner vision;

13 Enhancing life means good fortune;

14 Mind controlling spirit means inner strength.

15 "Beware old age in pride of manly might,"

16 For that means working against the Way.

17 "Work against the Way, die before your day."

COMMENT   Regarding lines 1–5 Wang Bi comments: "Having no demand nor desire, the infant does not provoke any of the ten thousand creatures." Su Che adds: "Being formless, *Dao* cannot be seen, much less harmed by anything. Men come to manifest themselves when the mind develops. After intention comes form; after form comes opposition and enmity. . . . Indifferent in its lack of desire, the infant's physique is at its perfection. When an external object presents itself, it lacks the consciousness to respond."[4]

In his chapter "Kengsang Chu" (name of a purported disciple of Laozi) Zhuangzi elaborates on the virtue of the infant: "The baby howls . . . yet . . . never gets hoarse . . . makes fists . . . yet its fingers never cramp. . . . It has no preference in the world of externals. To move without knowing where you are going, . . . riding along with [things] on the same wave—this is the basic rule of life preservation."[5]

Neither *xin,* "mind," nor *qi,* "spirit," in line 14 is a major term of the *Laozi.* In the chapter "In the World of Men" ("Renjian Shi") Zhuangzi describes the fasting of the mind: "Listening stops with the ears, the mind stops with recognition, but spirit is empty and waits on all things."[6] For the Zhuangzi Daoists, spirit is a higher consciousness or receptivity that the assertive, subjective mind cannot achieve. In the *Laozi,* however, spirit is a lesser power and has not superseded the mind.

The bonding of *qi* to *Dao* is a key theme of the *Xiang'er* commentary. *Qi* represents the physical vitality that humans and animals have in common. Thus the infant symbolizes men when still in the pre-socialized stage of life: he has acquired no language and belongs to the biological world. Regaining that state in a conscious register, the wise man regains the Way.

STANZA 56

1 Those who know it do not say it;
2 Those who say it do not know it.

    o   o   o

3 Those who know bar interaction,
4 Shut and seal the gates and doors;
5 They dull their keen edge and
6 Resolve their differences,
7 Reconcile the points of view
8 And blend with the lowly dust.
9 This we call sublime at-oneness.

    o   o   o

10 Favor affects them not,
11 Nor disfavor,
12 Neither advantage
13 Nor injury,
14 Neither honor
15 Nor dishonor.
16 Thus those who know are honored in the world.

COMMENT   The word *yan*, "say," in line 1 is mainly used to refer to organized speech, the statement of a position. The sage avoids exposing his advocacy; he takes no side and thus does not become one of a pair of opposites. Lines 3–7 describe the ways of interdicting conflict and disputation so that the ruler can keep his subjects free of knowledge and desire, hence free of conflicts.[1]

Gu Li thinks this stanza is addressed to a weakening nobility. "From the beginning of the Spring and Autumn era, conflicts among the slave-holding nobles . . . have led to many a bloody incident. . . . Laozi was particularly concerned by this, and his goal was to moderate these conflicts. . . . The overarching theme is 'balance or moderate major grievances' (stanza 79)." Zhang Songru comments: "Seeing contradiction, Laozi seeks harmony. This influenced Zhuangzi's relativism."

Su Che says that lines 3 and 4 describe blocking external influences and lines 5–8 describe inner cultivation, the achievement of disengaged impartiality. The phrase *he qi guang,* "reconcile the points of view" has not been convincingly explained. Waley says, "All glare tempered"; Chan and Lao say, "Soften the glare." These translations seem to follow the Heshang gong commentary, which says, "Though you have rare insight, blend it and make it seem dark and unknowing rather than allow it to dazzle."

The unique phrase in line 9, *xuantong,* "sublime at-oneness," occurs in Zhuangzi's chapter "Rifling Trunks." Following Waley's translation in stanza 56, Watson translates *xuantong* as "Mysterious Levelling," referring to the cessation of polemics among various philosophical schools.[2]

1   Rule kingdoms by right;

2   Wage war by deceit;

3   To win the world forsake ambition;

4   How do I know that this is so?

5   The more thou-shalt-nots for the world,

6   The more the people are deprived.[1]

7   The more devices that bring gain,

8   The more the clan and kingdom's bane.

9   The more that clever crafts expand,

10   The more strange artifacts abound.

11   The more the laws and writs declared,

12   The more that crime and violence spread.

13   Hence the wise in rule have said,

14   "May we under-govern and

15   The ruled uplift themselves.

16   May we remain inactive and

17   The ruled right themselves.

18   May we forsake ambition and

19   The ruled enrich themselves.

20   May we have no more desire

21   And the ruled keep their simple ways."[2]

COMMENT   This attack on ritual, invention, and law ends with an emphasis on the ruler's self *(wo)* as the standard for governing. Not law nor directive Confucian rule but self-restraining, self-effacing sagely rule will liberate the people, who then "of themselves" *(zi)* will prosper and enjoy good order. This becomes possible when the rulers "forsake ambition" *(wushi,* a phrase close in meaning to *wuwei).* Waley translates it "letting-alone."

The implicit opposition between the terms *fa,* law, and *wo,* self, in this *Laozi* stanza contrasts with other *Huangdi sijing* texts that reconcile *Dao* and law. They speak of the ruler as a creator and a follower of the law. "*Dao* gives birth to law. . . . He who controls the *Dao* gives birth to law and never dares to violate it."[3]

"Have no more desire" in the closing lines does not refer to biological desire, but rather to the socially created desire that drives economic ambition.

The last word of the stanza, *pu* (simple, primitive, pure, elemental), suggests the opening binoms of the next stanza: *men-men* (restrained and contained) and *chun-chun* (simple and wholesome). *Pu* also suggests the simple utopia described in stanza 80.

STANZA 58

1   Under rule restrained but caring[1]

2   Simple and wholesome stay the ruled;

3   But under rule that probes and prods

4   They connive and they contrive.

5   Good fortune stands beside ill fate;

6   Beneath good fortune ill fate hides.

7   Who can find the turning point?

8   For it there is no standard rule:

9   Rule reverses to exception,

10   Boon reverses to affliction,

11   For which men have lost direction

12   For a time of long duration.

13   This is why the wise who rule

14   Keep to the square but form no edge,

15   Gather gains but will not thrust,

16   Stay straight and true but cross no line;

17   And shed light but not to blind.[2]

COMMENT   As stanzas 40 and 42 also describe, the Way works by reverse motion through the dialectic of opposites in each thing. Only by holding fast to oneness can a person cope with the changes. Zhuangzi cites Laozi in his chapter "Kengsang Chu": "Can you embrace the one? Can you keep from losing it? Can you, without tortoise shell or divining stalks, foretell fortune and misfortune?"[3] According to Gu Li, the closing lines of this stanza could also mean one should stick to one's principles without sacrificing flexibility.[4]

Though not in the Guodian text, this stanza seems responsive to the previous stanza, which is in the Guodian. See the last point in the comment for stanza 57.

STANZA 59

1   For ruling men, for serving heaven.

2   Nothing surpasses having in store.

3   For it is having in store

4   That we call taking precaution.[1]

5   And taking precaution we call

6   Bent on amassing one's powers.

7   Bent on amassing one's powers

8   Means overcoming all obstacles.

9   Overcoming all obstacles

10   Means having no known turning point.

11   Having no known turning point[2]

12   Gives dominion over the kingdom.

13   The mother-source of this dominion

14   Yields staying power—

15   What is known as deep roots and strong base,

16   The Way of extended life and sustained reflection.[3]

COMMENT   The interpretation of this stanza depends on the word *se* in line 3, "having in store." *Se* means "reserving grain" but has usually been read as a metaphor for political control based on discipline over one's mental and physical powers. This has been the prevailing interpretation in both Chinese commentaries and English translations. Following Wang Bi's comment, however, Yin Zhenhuan develops the idea that *se* refers to giving priority to agriculture.[4] The reference in line 13 to the fruitful earth supports Yin's interpretation. Su Che does not follow Wang Bi's agricultural explanation and suggests that the qualities described in lines 14–17 of the previous stanza are instances of "having in store." In line 1 the word "heaven" *(tian)* is often interpreted naturalistically, as it is in the *Zhuangzi*.

This stanza is in the Guodian text, where line 1 has "provide" *(ji)* rather than "rule" *(zhi)*. "Provide" supports the interpretation of *se* (restraint) as *se* in the sense of "gathering in the harvest"—over the interpretation of Han Feizi, who reads *se* as garnering or conserving (the leader's) virtue or spiritual powers. The present translation, however, keeps to the received wording because of the surrounding stanzas, which contain advice to those in power.

STANZA 60

1   Rule a great state as you cook a small fish.

      o   o   o

2   Through the Way take a ruler's place in the world,

3   And the ghosts of the dead shall have no force.

4   Is it that they have no force?

5   Or that their force can do no harm?

6   That their force can do no harm?

7   Or that the wise lord does no harm?

8   Nor ghosts nor wise lord doing harm

9   To their joint virtue thus redounds.

COMMENT   Doing no harm, the wise lord leaves no wronged party to summon a ghost, no injustice proclaimed that the spirits of the dead must return to redress. This stanza is based both on the Mohist view of ghosts as agents of justice and on folk wisdom about the avenging role of the underworld. Mozi argues that ghosts descend to punish the evil and reward the good.

The phrase "great state" in line 1 is not seen earlier in the *Laozi.* Wang Bi says, commenting on this line, "The larger the kingdom, the quieter should the ruler be." Such a kingdom would present the specific problems of modernization, aggrandizement, and war-making that Laozi has been addressing all along. Wars are declared in the ancestral temple, and the sacred dead are summoned to bless the cause. "Cooking a small fish" represents minimal handling, which would include a minimum of official activity, war requisitions, regulations, imposts—all the activities that disturb agricultural work. The fish remains intact, uninjured; the metaphor suggests attentiveness to what is small, as well as gentleness toward small kingdoms (in addition to consideration for the farmers). Laozi's opposition to war and ritual are thus connected.

Fortune and misfortune generate one another; they do not come from the supernatural or the ancestral dead. Those who rule according to *Dao* are cognizant of this. Stanza 58 says, "Good fortune stands beside ill fate; / Beneath good fortune ill fate hides." Mozi took the first step in demystifying the spirits when he made them responsive to the deeds of all, not simply ancestral agents at the service of the aristocracy. Laozi goes a step farther in declaring that the dead will lose their power to affect the living when rulers rule by the Way. The Zhuangzi chapter "Mending the Inborn Nature" says, "At that time the *yin* and *yang* were harmonious and still; ghosts and spirits worked no mischief."[1] And the "Way of Heaven" chapter of the *Zhuangzi* says, "With a unified mind one can become king of the empire; then the ghosts will not plague."

This stanza, and indeed the entire *Laozi*, may be counted as one of the voices of protest against the idea that ghosts and spirits have power over humans. This is another way by which Laozi replaces historical time with natural time.

The opening line seems to have no connection to the remainder of the stanza and was probably an independent saying.

STANZA 61

1   A mighty kingdom stays downstream,

2   Female of this world below,

3   Where all courses intersect.

4   Dam holding still has ever conquered sire.

5   But to hold herself still

6   She must remain below.

7   By lying below a small kingdom

8   A great one takes it over.

9   By lying below a great kingdom

10   A small state is taken over.

11   By moving lower the greater takes over.

12   Lying low the smaller is taken over.

13   A great kingdom seeks no more

14   Than to absorb and protect.

15   A small state no more than to enter its service.

16   Thus for both to fulfill their desire

17   Lower must the greater lie.

COMMENT   The water imagery in this stanza evokes the closing lines of stanza 32, "The Way's a presence in the realm of men, / As valley streams join rivers, then the ocean," and also relates to the neighboring antiwar stanzas, 30 and 31. Stanza 60 addresses internal policy; this one, external affairs. The two stanzas seem to form a set. Neither is found in the Guodian text.

In this stanza Laozi urges great rulers to find a benign balance in relation to unequals, both stronger and weaker, rather than pursue a course of conquest. Gu Li argues that such a position reflects the late Spring and Autumn political context rather than a middle or late Warring States context. The stanza fits into a world of hegemonic *(ba)* or league-forming *(meng)* rulers who need to expand their blocs, rather than the late-third-century B.C. world of large kingdom alliances that were made when most of the smaller kingdoms had already been devoured by the greater.[1] However, one could also argue that Laozi's prescriptions for international peace are hardly different from Mencius's. In Mencius 1B.3 a king of Qi asks, "Is there a proper way to interact with the neighboring kingdoms?" Mencius replies, "Only the humane [ruler] can lead his greater kingdom to serve a smaller one. . . . When we have a great kingdom serving a smaller one it shows a love of heaven; when we have a smaller serving a greater it shows an awe of heaven." For both Laozi and Mencius the fate of the smaller kingdoms of the realm was a critical issue.

STANZA 62

1   A midden for the myriad,[1]

2   The Way is sacred to men of merit

3   And a safeguard to all who do wrong.

4   Fine words may buy high station,

5   Fine deeds win men's acclaim,[2]

6   But why turn from those who do wrong?

7   For when the son of heaven is enthroned,

8   And his three elder statesmen are installed,

9   Better to counsel them in the Way

10   Than ride an envoy's four-horse coach

11   Heralded by the jade disc of state.

12   Why did men of old honor the Way?

13   Has it not been said, "Through the Way

14   Shall right be found, wrongdoers spared"?

15   For this the world honors the Way.

COMMENT   Nothing from the sacrifice is considered waste; all leavings go to the sacred midden, much as the Way receives all people and all things. "[T]he wise know how to salvage men / And . . . things" (stanza 27). The one who can teach a king how to transcend contradictions, to use the negative as well as the positive, is worth more to the kingdom than the tribute of the rich and the acclaim of men.

STANZA 63

1   Do what is undone;

2   Serve the unserved;

3   Savor what lacks savor;

4   Make bigger smaller, more less;

5   Repay a wrong with friendly favor.[1]

  o o o

6   Forestall trouble when it's easy to.

7   Act on the major when it's still minor.

8   For this world's troubles start with simple things,

9   And major matters rise from little ones.

10 Thus the wise, not making much of them,

11 Can always see their great works through.

  o o o

12 But "lightly granted rarely honored";

13 And much too easy means much trouble.

14 Even the wisest looks for the trouble ahead,

15 And ends up with the trouble spared.

COMMENT Lines 1–5 describe how a ruler moves in a direction contrary to expectations and self-interest in order to minimize conflict. *Wei* ("do" in line 1) is connected in stanza 3 with *zhi*, govern, and means govern in the phrase *weibang* in the *Analects*. *Wuwei* describes action that has so little personal purpose, so little subjective dimension, that it is highly responsive to objective circumstances, which are always changing. Thus the disinterested actor can perceive the becoming in the existing.

The first line reads: *wei wuwei*. Perhaps this ambiguous three-word phrase implies its sequel, *wu buwei,* in stanza 48: "No end pursued, no end ungained." Most translations suggest "act without act-ing" or some variation thereof for *wei wuwei,* but a verb-object con-struction is more likely. Stanza 3 of this translation reads: "acting . . . without taking the lead." Other meanings of the semantically com-plex word *wei* include acting for a subjective gain or purpose, and acting in an artificial manner. The phrase *wei wuwei* has the power and ambiguity of Hamlet's "To be or not to be," and possibly the same syntax too. If lines 1–3 are translated "to act or not to act; to serve or not to serve; to savor or not to savor," then the rest of the stanza would consist of the bases for making these choices.

Lines 1–3 probably critique Confucian bureaucrats, for whom self-cultivation, social ambition, and banqueting were primary. Laozi limits ambition and appetite, humbly grants the small and the few their due, and disdains prideful retaliations. These are the preconditions for undertaking the tasks the rest of the stanza enu-merates. The Confucian model is to develop a world order out of the educated statesmen *(junzi)* in government service, based on the logic of "from the self to the other": "as you establish and achieve for the self, establish and achieve for the other" (*Analects* 6.28). Laozi, on the other hand, like Mozi, sees the development of the self and its sphere as an obstacle to the ordering of the world not as a precondition for it.

The Guodian text of this stanza is much briefer, consisting of only lines 1–3, the first half of line 4, and lines 13–15.[2]

STANZA 64

1   What's stable is easy to secure,

2   The unmanifest to plan against,[1]

3   The fragile to splinter,

4   The incipient to dissolve.

5   Act before events occur:

6   Decision can prevent disorder.

7   A tree of girth

8   Grows from a twig.

9   A nine-tier tower

10   From a basket of earth;

11   And a thousand-mile journey

12   Begins where one stands.

     o   o   o

13   Those who take the lead shall fail.

14   Those who cling lose hold.

15   This is why men of wisdom,

16   Taking no lead, do not fail,

17   Not clinging, do not lose hold.

18   How often do people, assuming a task,

19   Ruin it at the verge of success?

20   Hence the saying,

21   "Careful at the end as at the start,

22   And your task shall not abort."

23   This is why the worldly wise

24   Seek what others do not seek,

25   "Prize not goods hard to find,"

26   Learn what others do not learn:[2]

27   Redeem the wrongs many have done.

28   In this way support and sustain

29   The self-becoming of the myriad,

30   And do not presume to act upon them.

COMMENT   Explaining the final lines of this stanza, Han Feizi tells the following story:

> A commoner of the kingdom of Song came into possession of a rich piece of gem ore and offered to present it to Zihan [a minister in the kingdom of Zheng]. When Zihan refused the gift, the commoner said, "This treasure should go to a noble man, not to an unimportant one." Zihan replied, "You treasure the treasure. I treasure not accepting your stone." Thus the commoner valued the stone, but Zihan valued not desiring [yu] the stone. This explains Laozi's lines 25 and 26: "Seek [yu] what others do not seek; prize not goods hard to find."[3]

The last lines of this stanza seem to have influenced the passage in "Xinshi" (Conditions and circumstances) in the *Guanzi* that says, "When [the ruler] achieves the way of heaven, his undertakings seem like those of nature itself . . . no one realizes that he is taking action." The opening lines were adapted in the first chapter of the *Guanzi*, "Mumin" (Guiding the people): "Those who possess the Way are able to prepare for trouble before it has begun to take form." Both these *Guanzi* chapters seem to have been heavily influenced by the *Laozi*.[4]

With line 13 of this stanza part one of the Guodian *Laozi* ends; the remainder of the stanza is placed at the end of the third and last part. Presumably, then, these were separate passages for the Guodian editor-scribe. But why? In the view of scholar Gao Chenyang, this separation suggests that the Guodian text was selected from a larger text. He writes: "This stanza first says that when things are in a quiescent or incipient condition or are undergoing the initial changes, they are easy to deal with. The stanza then proceeds to emphasize acting before events occur, speaking metaphorically of the tree that grows from a slip. Finally the stanza speaks of being as careful at the end as at the start." If the Guodian editor broke up a whole stanza, Gao Chenyang suggests, then perhaps we should look at the entire Guodian text as excerpts, rather than as the original *Laozi*.[5]

A different approach to this stanza is taken by Yin Zhenhuan. He sees no connection between the two halves of the stanza and thinks they were originally separate stanzas or statements.[6]

1   Those of old who pursued the Way

2   Never meant to make their people see;

3   Their purpose was to keep them unaware.

4   The people are harder to manage

5   For knowing things.

6   To have the learned govern the kingdom

7   Is a bane to the kingdom.

8   Not to have them

9   Is a boon to the kingdom.

10   Know always that this double dictum

11   Defines a guide to judgment,

12   Which when firmly fixed in mind

13   May be called sublime virtue.

14   Such virtue, deep and reaching far,

15   In counter-motion like all things,

16   Achieves congruence with the Way.

COMMENT   Mencius (3A4.8) describes how the sage-kings of antiquity first taught (*jiao*) the people to sow and reap and then appointed a minister of education to teach the people about social relations and their attendant ethical codes so that the people's virtue (*de*) would be stimulated. Laozi opposes the entire Confucian principle of government by education.

There are relevant passages in the *Analects* as well to which this stanza may refer. *Analects* 8.9 says, "What the people may be made to follow they may not be made to understand." This passage is sometimes adduced as a parallel to stanza 65 of the *Laozi*, a variant on the theme of keeping the people ignorant. However, Confucius may simply be acknowledging the limits of the people in a particular situation rather than, uncharacteristically, opposing teaching the people. More typical of Confucian thought, *Analects* 13.9 speaks of teaching (*jiao*) the people after seeing that they have multiplied and grown wealthy. This passage comports well with the tenor of the *Analects,* with its advocacy of open enrollment, learning for government service, and lifelong devotion to education.

This stanza and stanzas 63 and 64 are thematically related to stanza 3: "Thus under a wise man's rule / Blank are their minds." Chinese commentators are divided over the meaning of *yu,* "unaware," in line 3 of this stanza. Does Laozi mean to keep the people ignorant or merely simple, to deceive them or to guide them back to an elemental life? Gu Li takes a power-politics standpoint and favors the former; those taking a utopian, simplify-society view, such as Chen Guying and Zhang Songru, favor the latter.

This stanza is not found in the Guodian manuscript.

STANZA 66

1   Why is it that the rivers and the ocean,

2   Like kings, can lead the many valley streams?

3   Knowing how to stay below, they

4   Draw to them the many higher streams.

5   For this reason wise and worldly rulers,

6   Wishing to remain above their people,[1]

7   Need to stay below by what they say;

8   Or if they wish to go before their people,

9   They need to take their place behind.

10   Beneath such rule the people feel no weight;

11   Such leadership the people feel no threat.[2]

12   All the world rejoices and supports them

13   And never tries to cast such rulers off.

14   Is it not because they will not strive

15   That no one in this world can strive with them?

COMMENT   Laozi reverses the top-down model of Confucian leadership here. In *Analects* 12.19 Confucius says: "The virtue of the true prince *(junzi)* is like the wind that bends lesser men below as if they were grass." Laozi's rulers, who "take as theirs the people's mind" (stanza 49) leave the people saying, "This was no one's doing but our own" (stanza 17). Lying low, Laozi's leaders never seek high station nor exert power from above.

In the Guodian manuscript this stanza follows stanza 19 and may be a logical continuation of 19's emphasis on simplicity and lack of desire, presumably in those who rule. Of the eighty-one received stanzas, stanza 66 is the last found in the Guodian text.

Wang, "king," in line 2 was defined early on by the homophone "to draw toward," so the king was someone who attracted a wide following because of his moral charisma. In *Mencius* the term is exalted by connection with *Dao* in the recurring term "kingly way" *(wangdao)*, which described idealized governing by a virtuous king.

1   "All the world declares me great."

2   Be great but do not seem to be.

3   For it is seeming not to be

4   That makes you great.

5   Otherwise, by seeming so,

6   You'd long ago have ceased to matter.

      o   o   o

7   We have always our triple treasure,[1]

8   Which we rely upon and cherish:

9   "A mother's heart, a frugal hand, and

10   No drive to boldly lead this world."

11   A brave heart takes a mother's heart,

12   A giving hand a frugal hand;

13   And one who will not lead to serve

14   As sacred elder of this world.

15   Forsaking love for bravery,

16   Frugal hand for giving hand,

17   Staying back for leading forth

18   Mean entering the gates of death.

19   A mother's heart holds battle lines

20   And also makes defenses sure.

21   The man whom heaven means to keep[2]

22   It protects with mother-heart.

COMMENT   In the *Laozi,* the pronoun *wo* (I, we) refers either to those in power or to the author. In line 1 of this stanza *wo* probably means the ruler. Perhaps the first line is intended as the speech of a ruler and the second line as the author's reply. Unlike all other texts, the Mawangdui included, Wang Bi has put the word *Dao* after *wo* in line 1. Such a construction, *wo Dao* (our Way), resembles the construction *wu Dao* in *Analects* 4.15. Though many translations have followed Wang Bi's emendation, modifying *Dao* with a personal pronoun is not compatible with other uses of the word *Dao* in this book. Lines 1 and 2 are subject to extreme variation of interpretation in commentary and translation.

This stanza speaks of maternal rather than patriarchal authority. The Confucian patriarch teaches his people (who are his "children") to follow his example *(xiao)* and be true to him (*xiao*, filial piety). But the beings created by *Dao* can only be themselves (*ziran*, self-becoming). They do not resemble or imitate the *Dao* that produced them, nor revere it as a superior, nor stand in its debt, even though they learn from it and apply its laws. The same maternal authority, not the power of the ancestors, guarantees the security of the political ruler.

Under-translation of the term *ci* (translated here as "mother's heart"), which refers only to the love between parent and child—usually from the parental side—has led to a weakening of the force of this stanza in English versions. In Warring States usage, *ci* may contrast with *xiao*, filial piety, as "parent love" or may serve as a reinforcing adjective to *xiao: ci-xiao*, kind-hearted filial piety. Given the thematic emphasis of the *Laozi*, however, "mother-love" seems preferable to "parent-love" as a translation. Moreover, Han Feizi's comment on this stanza in the "Jie Lao" starts with the phrase *cimu*, loving mother.

This stanza weaves the theme of staying low and holding back in stanza 66 together with the earlier theme of keeping to the female principle in stanza 28. In the present stanza Laozi links both themes to military strategy and finally to heaven's protection. Heaven does not mandate *(ming)* a male sovereign in Laozi's text, but it does see to the safety of a ruler that lives by its principles. The idea of an attentive heaven appears only in the non-Guodian stanzas.[3] For this and all remaining stanzas—stanzas 67 through 81—there is no Guodian counterpart. Stanzas 67, 68, and 69 form a unified set.

Lines 19–20 have two variant readings: "With ci form battle lines and you will hold the front," and "With ci engage in battle and you shall win." The second is popular in modern Chinese editions and English translations but seems overconfident, given Laozi's recessive style, so I have chosen to translate this line according to the B-text reading of the Mawangdui *Laozi*. This reading also accords better with Laozi's preference for defensive war—war only if war cannot be avoided.

STANZA 68

1   Warriors who excel do not parade;
2   Commanders who excel do not anger;
3   Victors who excel don't lightly engage;
4   Skilled managers of men are humble:
5   This defines the power of no-conflict,
6   The way to manage men's strength,
7   The union with heaven, the acme of old.

COMMENT   The previous stanza emphasized the maternal virtues; this stanza complements it by emphasizing their male form.

According to this stanza, restraint is the qualification for becoming an ideal ruler, like Wenwang (King Wen, "the civil king"). The closing line has the phrase *peitian* (matching heaven), which is also used in the *Book of Odes,* in odes "Wenwang" and "Si Wen." A marital term, *peitian* means becoming a partner to heaven, hence, heaven's mandated representative. This borrowing from the *Odes* is another case of incorporating Confucian political terms into the Daoist agenda. In the *Book of Odes* the virtue of Wenwang qualifies him to receive the mandate of heaven and overthrow the reigning Shang dynasty. Wenwang came to be considered the founding emperor of the Zhou house, though it was his son, Wuwang, "the martial king," who conquered Shang by force of arms.

Gu (old, ancient) appears in line 7 in some texts. This word is used sixty-two times on its own in the *Laozi* and another thirteen times in combination. Such frequency marks the author's repeated gazing back to a remote time when the ills and evils he describes did not exist. *Gu* may refer to a pre-Zhou (i.e., Shang) period, or simply to an imagined time of simplicity. Laozi may have lived and written in the kingdom of Chu, which had roots in the Shang and maintained a tradition of resisting Zhou power.

STANZA 69

1   Those who wage war often say,[1]

2   "We prefer response to invitation,

3   The span withdrawn to the inch gained."

4   This is formation that does not go forward,

5   Deflection with hand unraised,

6   The firm grip that holds no sword,

7   And the thrust that cannot be countered.[2]

8   But "having no foe" is the greatest threat.

9   It leads to the loss of our triple treasure.

10   Once battle is joined, who gives way wins.

COMMENT   One of the meanings of *wuwei* in a military context is defensive preparedness. A passive, defensive mode is more effective than an active, aggressive one. And a defensive psychology is essential for survival—a point that is made directly in line 8's warning against self-confident disdain of an enemy. Mencius's famous formulation goes: "Without enemy kingdoms and external dangers the state will fall" (6B.15).

Some scholars see in *bao*, "treasure," in line 9 a reference to stanza 67: if we imagine we have no enemy, we will lose our caring (for the people), our frugality, and our reluctance to take a (military) initiative. In line 10, most texts have *ai*, mourn, instead of *xiang*, which is a near-homonym to *rang* (give way, yield). With *ai*, this line has entered the Chinese language as a common saying: "soldiers who sorrow prevail," in the spirit of stanza 31. However, "yield" seems to make better sense in this context than "sorrow," and there are a number of other examples of textual interchanges between the two words due to graphic similarity.

The terms *zhu*, host, and *ke*, guest, are explored in the "Contending Clans" section of *Sixteen Canons:* "When something should be done and is not done, the heavenly clockwork rolls on around, and man is left in the passive position [as guest]." "Contending Clans" departs from Laozi's preference for the guest or reactive role and treats both proactive and reactive roles as having their proper time.[3]

STANZA 70

1   What we say is easy to know

2   And easy to do,

3   But the world does not know its worth

4   And does not act upon it.

5   Though we speak with an ancestral sanction

6   And serve on high authority,[1]

7   Yet this remains unknown

8   And so we remain unknown.

9   And the less that we are known,

10   More precious our followers.

11   For this reason men of wisdom

12   Wear rough garb and the gem in the heart.

COMMENT   Most scholars and translators place this stanza in the biographical category (stanzas 20, 41) as an instance of the author lamenting the failure of his teachings. In these lines Laozi is more pessimistic than in stanza 41, where some follow his teachings and others scoff. Invoking ancestral sanction and high authority are unusual for this text and again suggest a willingness to adopt Confucian rhetoric. The metaphor of hiding the gem (i.e., talent) within occurs several times in the *Analects*. In *Analects* 17.1, for example, Confucius is chided for not placing his talents at the disposal of the ruler: "Is that what you call 'benevolent'—holding the gem within and letting your kingdom go astray?"

STANZA 71

1   To recognize ignorance comes first;
2   Not to know to know this will cause harm:
3   Harm that the wise are spared
4   Because they recognize it.
5   Only by recognizing the harm
6   Can one be spared.[1]

COMMENT   There are a number of Warring States references to the opening lines of this stanza, and the majority of commentators and translators follow an elaboration in the *Lüshi chunqiu*, "Bielei" chapter: "To know [that one] does not know is best /
Not to know but to assume that one knows causes harm." There is
no reason, however, to restrict Laozi's formula here with a pronoun. It is as important to recognize another's ignorance as it is to
recognize one's own.

Many commentaries make a connection to *Analects* 2.17: "Let
knowing it be taken for knowing it, ignorance for ignorance."
Many commentaries and translations of this stanza have been influenced by the verb-*wei*-verb grammar of *Analects* 2.17 and thus
present Laozi as talking about knowledge taken for ignorance and
vice versa. Laozi seems to be playing with Confucius's formula by
inverting it verbally, though arriving at a similar conclusion. In the
Analects, knowledge *(zhi)* is something valuable to be gained by
learning *(xue)*. Laozi opposes knowledge as no more than a qualification for bureaucratic recruitment. In this stanza, however, a positive value for knowledge—suggesting knowledge of the Way—is
suggested by the previous and succeeding stanzas.

The grammar of the opening line—*zhi buzhi* (literally, "know,
not know," translated here as "to recognize ignorance")—leaves
room for many interpretations. If we compare the grammar of *yu*

buyu and *xue buxue*—"seek what others do not seek," "learn what others do not learn"—in stanza 64, then a verb-object grammar seems best. And if line 1 has a verb-object structure, normally line 2 follows the pattern. Another translation of the opening lines according to this grammar would read: "To know the unknown is best / Not to know the known harms." This reading resembles a line in the *Daoyuan* text in the *Huangdi sijing:* "Know what others are unable to know" *(zhi ren zhi suo buneng zhi).* However, none of the major translators adopt this Machiavellian reading.

Su Che reads the lines differently again. "To understand [the value of] not knowing is the highest; not to understand [the danger of] knowing is an affliction."[2] This interpretation seeks to preserve consistency with earlier admonitions against knowledge. To Su Che, Laozi is warning against distorting his rejection of knowledge into a complete alienation of society. Laozi advocates, rather, a different way of working in society—principled and self-effacing—and a different kind of society, but not a rejection of society. Therefore, certain forms of knowledge are necessary; knowledge as Laozi redefines it approaches *ming,* insight.

In Wei Yuan's edition stanzas 70 and 71 are grouped as one. He reads the opening lines as a continuation of stanza 70's lament of the world's ignorance of the Way, which requires the wise man to hide his knowledge in humble garb.

STANZA 72

1   When people dread not the powers that be,

2   A greater dread is on the way.

   o   o   o

3   Encroach not on their domain;

4   Do not burden down their lives.

5   Only of those who bear bearing

6   Will the people bear the burden.

7   This is why wise men who govern

8   Know themselves, show themselves not,

9   Conserve themselves, esteem themselves not:

10 Rejecting these, preferring those.

COMMENT   Does this stanza on preserving political authority speak for the ruled or for those who rule? Scholars hold opposing views. Some see Laozi as a populist and potential revolutionary; others see Laozi as a cunning adviser to a slave-owning (i.e., labor-owning) aristocracy. Taking a middle position between the two, Gu Li argues that Laozi represents former or weakened labor-owning aristocrats who see the imminent supplantation of their form of rule by rising land-owning entrepreneurs. For Gu Li, therefore, Laozi is an urgent voice of reformist admonition speaking to the aristocrats of presumably older, smaller kingdoms.[1]

It is likely that the first two lines are a short aphorism rather than part of the stanza, since they are set off in Mawangdui A. Yin Zhenhuan cites the well-known *Zuozhuan* passage: "Only men of virtue can exert authority with tolerance. The lesser mode is that of severity. Because fire burns, the people regard it with dread and few die of it. Because water is soft and gentle, the people trifle with it for amusement and many die of it. Tolerance is truly difficult to govern by."[2]

The final ten stanzas of the *Dao De Jing*, 72–81, develop the theme of gentleness and fairness in rule. Were these stanzas added to an earlier set to counter Legalist applications of Daoist thought—to argue for a more humane less policy-directed statecraft?

STANZA 73

1   Be brave in daring: kill or be killed;

2   Be brave in not daring: live and let live;

3   One of the two brings gain, one harm.

4   But which man knows what heaven condemns,

5   What precedents it's guided by?[1]

       o   o   o

6   The way of heaven masters all:

7   It prevails though striving not,

8   It replies though speaking not,

9   Comes although uncalled,

10   And gives good counsel though affected not.[2]

11   Heaven's net, cast far and wide,

12   Seems slack yet nothing slips outside.

COMMENT   Su Che comments: "The world contemplates heaven with eyes and ears, seeing one corner but not recognizing the whole. When good men meet with disaster and evildoers enjoy good fortune, who has not suspected that heaven's net lets too much slip through? Only by grasping the whole process from beginning to end, comprehending the twists and turns, can one appreciate that nothing escapes the net despite its vast stretch."[3] The word "precedents" in line 5 is the translation of *gu,* a word derived from *gu* in the sense of "ancient." It means what is already well established, a basis. The term poses a challenge to two other forms of well-established authority through which judgments are reached and punishments administered: the ancestors and the law. Laozi warns that heaven's judgments transcend and supersede those of humans.

1   If the people fear not even death itself,

2   How can execution frighten them?

3   If they are in constant fear of death,

4   And we seize and put to death

5   Committers of crimes, then who would dare?

6   But to keep the folk in constant fear,[1]

7   Keep the master executioner near.

8   Let none kill in his stead, for that would be

9   To wield the knife in the master's stead—

10   And no one who would for the master stand

11   Escapes with an uninjured hand.

COMMENT   These grim and cynical injunctions are set off but also necessitated by its gentler neighbors, stanzas 73 and 75. The placement of Laozi's biography together with that of the legalist Han Feizi in Sima Qian's *Shiji* may reflect the influence of this stanza. But many commentators, unwilling to see Laozi as a harsh proto-Legalist, have understood "executioner" to mean heaven's judgment on wrongdoers. Modern scholar Jiang Xichang follows this interpretation. If that indeed is the sense, then it follows that the ruler who employs capital punishment is usurping heaven's role and will injure himself.

If, however, Laozi is confronting the essential questions of statecraft in stanzas 73–76, in this stanza he may only be warning the ruler (the "we" of line 4) not to drive the people to desperation but to protect their livelihoods so that they will value their lives and thus accept his rule. Laozi may also want the ruler to distance himself personally from the necessary cruelties of suppressing crime, because ultimately the ruler bears that responsibility.[2] In the words of the noted Song dynasty commentator Fan Yingyuan, "This stanza means that when people violate the laws in their struggle for gain, it is because their leaders aggressively pursue their own excessive desires. The leaders only need to minimize their desires in a spirit of clear-sighted tranquillity and they will enable the people to turn towards civilized conduct on their own with no resort to death penalties."[3] This comment applies to the next stanza as well.

This stanza is a variation on a similar theme in *Analects* 12.19. In reply to the question, "What do you think of killing the lawless to attract the lawful?" Confucius said, "When you hold political authority, why use the death penalty? Seek what is good and useful and the people will be good and useful. The virtue of the true prince is like the wind that bends lesser men below as if they were grass."

STANZA 75

1   The people lack for food

2   When those above them overtax;

3   That is why they lack.

4   And the people can't be ruled

5   When those above them serve themselves.

6   That is why they can't be ruled.

    o   o   o

7   And when the people death defy

8   It is but to make their lives secure —[1]

9   That is why.

10   Worthier far than living royally

11   Those who live not for themselves.

COMMENT   *Analects* 12.9 records a conversation between Duke Ai, the patriarch of Lu, and You Ruo, a disciple of Confucius. You Ruo was urging the duke to make do with a tax rate of 10 percent. The patriarch replied that even 20 percent was insufficient for his purposes. You Ruo said, "If the people lack for means, with whom will your highness share your surplus?" Duke Ai ruled Lu from 495 – 94 to 470 – 69 B.C.

Military strategist Sunzi spells out the extraordinary costs of war: "[A]nd so the internal and external expenses, providing for diplomatic guests and dignitaries, glues and paints for repair, supplying chariots and armor come to a thousand pieces of gold a day before an army of ten thousand can be raised and readied."[2]

There is a division of interpretation among modern scholars regarding this stanza. Some see it as representing a popular opposition to the exploitation of rulers; others see Laozi as a reform-minded member of the ruling aristocracy intent on reminding those in power what happens to those who abuse the people.

STANZA 76

1. Man alive is tender, gentle,
2. Hard and fast in death.
3. Living plants are tender, fragile,
4. Dry and frail in death.
5. For fast and hard are marks of dying,
6. And gentle, tender marks of life.
7. Strength in arms brings destruction,
8. As the strong branch will be broken.
9. Let strength and might be put below,
10. And tender, gentle in control.

COMMENT   This stanza uses physiology and botany to lead into a comment on military tactics and governance—a pattern resembling the *xing* and *bi,* the "thought-provoking analogies," often opening the poems in the *Book of Odes (Shijing).*

The emphasis here is on life as sacred, rather than on the dead. The lives of human beings, as one of the ten thousand, are to be measured by season only, by natural time, not by generation, which is socially measured time. Thus Daoist thought is distinguished from Confucian and Mohist, which stress hereditary continuity through patriarchal social organization as the basis for the domination of other people and of the natural world of the ten thousand. Lines 9 and 10 suggest the superiority of the female or maternal principle, that is to say, the biological or reproductive over the social or generational.

STANZA 77

1   Heaven's Way, like unto a bow full-drawn—

2   Low end raised, top bent down—

3   Subtracts from the have-mores

4   And supplies those in want.

5   Heaven's Way—to supply who wants

6   By taking from the have-mores—

7   Is not the Way of men,

8   Who take from those in need

9   To serve those who have more.

10   Who will use the surplus to serve this world below?

11   None but men of the Way.

12   Wise rulers for this reason

13   Act without self-satisfaction,

14   For their deeds shun recognition

15   To conceal their contribution.

COMMENT   As the Song commentator Lü Jifu implies, the archer draws the bow to launch the arrow, not to raise the bow's lower end or lower its upper end. So also heaven, a bowlike vault, creates all things without partiality. Those who rule should imitate heaven's universal embrace.[1]

Marksmanship is a stock Confucian metaphor for personal responsibility in leadership. The archer has only himself to blame if his shot is not true. For Mencius, leaders must project their virtuous influence to attain the goal of humane government; if this goal is not reached, they are to blame. The use of archery in this stanza may also suggest sublimated rivalry, as in *Analects* 3.7: "The princely man will not contend, except in marksmanship, which he cannot avoid. He ascends the shooting mound with deferential salutations;

steps down when done and drinks the penalty cup. Such contending is indeed princely." More generally, the bow stands for warlike competition. Laozi uses the bow as a new metaphor for the principle of *jun*, equity in distribution. The word *jun*, meaning fairly shared, is found once in *Laozi* and once in the *Analects*. *Analects* 16.1 says, "It is said that what the rulers of kingdoms and of clans need fear is not having too little but having it unfairly shared." Stanza 32 speaks of a time when heaven's bounty was shared fairly among the people; the present stanza develops the theme of stanza 75, which critiques economic imbalance.

STANZA 78

1   What more gentle in this world than water?

2   Yet nothing better conquers hard and strong.

3   What else could take its place?

4   Gentle conquers strong, and tender hard.

5   Well-known as this is to all the world,

6   Who has proven able to apply it?

7   Wiser men accordingly have said,

8   "He who for the kingdom's sake bears shame

9   Earns the name—master of the shrine.

10   He who for the kingdom bears ill-fortune

11   Earns the name of king of all the world."

12   How untrue words of truth appear to be.

[handwritten marginalia: "be gentle but conquer — be hard & strong?"]

[handwritten marginalia: "ironic —"]

COMMENT   Distinguishing "master of the shrine" from "king of all the world," Gu Li suggests that the former is likely to refer to the ruler of a kingdom, the latter to the son of heaven of the royal Zhou court, that is, the titular universal sovereign. Gu Li cites the *Zuozhuan* text under Xuangong 15 (594 B.C.), which says, "As streams and marshes contain filth, and hilly woods harbor deadly beasts, and fine stones have hidden flaws, so the lord of the kingdom carries detritus."[1]

Modern scholar Gao Heng suggests a link between this stanza and *Analects* 20.1, in which the ruler says, "If we have personally committed an offense, my domains are not responsible; if somewhere in my domains an offense is committed, the blame rests with us."[2]

STANZA 79

1   When great wrongs resolved

2   Leave further wrongs behind—

3   What good will come of that?

4   When wise men hold the left half-tally pledge,

5   They do not press their debtors for their debts.

6   Men of virtue hold the tally pledge;

7   Men lacking virtue work pursuing claims.

8   Heaven's way does not show kinship favor

9   But rather joins with good and decent men.

COMMENT   This stanza on grievance has seemed to a number of modern scholars the proper place for the famous fragment traditionally located in stanza 63: "Repay a wrong with friendly favor." Chen Guying, for example, puts the fragment in line 3. The absence of the line in stanza 63 of the Guodian text strengthens the argument for moving it somewhere else, if not to this stanza.

Laozi's opposition to revenge is part and parcel of his opposition to striving and competing. One early Han text speaks of revenge as abundant in the Spring and Autumn period.[1] Mencius (7B.2) says that there were no just wars in the Spring and Autumn period. Mozi, too, describes the endless warring between clan and clan, kingdom and kingdom in his chapter on universal love ("Jianai"). With regard to conflict, Laozi wants to prevent a wrong before it becomes a "great wrong," for even when resolved, great wrongs never fail to leave a legacy of further wrongs.

Following the theme of stanza 77, this stanza likens the wise ruler to a creditor who would rather accept a loss than press for the return of what he lends. The creditor and the debtor each hold half of a split tally. When the debtor repays, the tallies are rejoined. If the debtor comes voluntarily, then there is no grievance. Those who pursue their claims — or overtax their people — only succeed in creating grievances.

The closing line seems to accommodate the Confucian viewpoint: "Heaven joins with good and decent men." However, the tally itself is indifferent and favors no one. Heaven favors whoever tallies with heaven.

Heaven has no favorites, nor has it enemies. In the Mawangdui text, stanza 79 is the final stanza, since 80 and 81 follow stanza 66. In stanza 79 the editor seems to extend an olive branch to the Confucian and Mohist schools, both of which argue for a heaven that is responsive to humans. The graph for *yu* in line 9, here translated "joins," shows two hands giving and two receiving. Perhaps there is an implication that heaven makes the generous ruler whole, repaying all he has given to others. Most commentators interpret *yu* to mean to lend aid, to provide for, to be with.

This stanza emphasizes the word *ren* (human, man) rather than the word *min*, which means the common people — referring to economics or occupation. Stanzas 74 and 75 are *min*-oriented; stanzas 76 – 79 are *ren*-oriented. *Ren* may include *min* as a subcategory, but if the context is social, *ren* usually means those of higher standing, men of importance, personages. Accordingly, Gu Li and others read this stanza as a plea for compromise among the rulers *(ren)* of the kingdoms, rather than as a critique of those rulers from the vantage of the ruled *(min)*.

STANZA 80

1 Keep the kingdom small, its people few;

2 Make sure they have no use for tools

3 That do the work of tens or hundreds.

4 Nor let the people travel far

5 And leave their homes and risk their lives.

6 Boat or cart, if kept at all, best not to ride;

7 Shield and blade best not to show.

8 Guide them back to early times,

9 When knotted cords served for signs,

10 And they took relish in their food

11 And delight in their dress,

12 Secure in their dwellings,

13 Content in their customs,

14 Although a neighbor kingdom stood in view

15 And the barnyard cries of cocks and dogs

16 Echoed from village to village,

17 Their folk would never traffic to and fro—

18 Never, to the last of their days.

COMMENT   This stanza and the next are found in the Mawangdui texts following stanza 66. The image of an ideal, simplified
society seems to follow from the themes of the ideal people who
are kept simple and ignorant (stanza 65) and the ideal, self-effacing
rulers (stanza 66). So the placement of this stanza in the Mawangdui texts has a certain logic, though its position as stanza 80 in the
received text, culminating the preceding social criticism stanzas, is
also understandable.

Stanza 80 pulls together the topics of stanzas 72–79, which deal
with gentle rule and social justice. The self-sufficient, autarkic vil-

lage world Laozi idealizes also recapitulates earlier warnings against technology, trade, and bureaucracy. Perhaps Laozi is harking back to the time before the Zhou conquest of the Shang, when many tiny kingdoms dotted the Yellow and Huai river basins—a world that predated the process of cultural and economic integration of the embryonic "China." The *Zhuangzi* cites this stanza in the chapter "Rifling Trunks," which speaks of an "age of perfect virtue."[1]

The transformation of this ancient order is described in ode 237, "Mian." The last two stanzas of "Mian" celebrate road building in the early Zhou period, which was followed by conquests among the surrounding peoples. This marked the beginning of imperial expansion and integration.

This stanza is probably not too far in time from the mature Mencius, who uses the same imagery of cocks and dogs to describe the economic sufficiency of the glorious ancient kingdoms of Xia and the houses of Yin and Zhou (*Mencius* 2A.1.10).[2]

STANZA 81

1   Words to trust are not refined.

2   Words refined are not to trust.

3   Good men are not gifted speakers.

4   Gifted speakers are not good.

5   Experts are not widely learned;

6   The widely learned not expert.

   o   o   o

7   Wise rulers for themselves keep naught,

8   Yet gain by having done for all,

9   Have more for having freely shared;

10   Do good not harm is heaven's Way;

11   The wise act for and not against.

COMMENT   This final stanza appears to be a synthesis of Confucian and Daoist political wisdom. The opposition of self *(ji)* and other *(ren)* in lines 7–9, so characteristic of the *Analects* and *Mencius,* occurs in the *Laozi* only here. Moreover, the criticism of eloquence recalls the complaints in the *Analects* about cunning or artful speech *(qiaoyan)* and sophists *(yingren),* whose false learning and rhetoric are a threat to political order. In *Analects* 13.27, men of humanity are described as *nuo,* reticent. Finally, in this stanza wide learning *(bo)* is affirmed; in the *Analects* wide learning is advised if disciplined through ritual.

However, there is a textual variation for line 3. In the received text the word for eloquence in argument *(bian,* translated here as "gifted speakers") has replaced the word "many" found in the Mawangdui texts. Does this mean that Laozi's original complaint was against the paucity of good men in office, but that an authoritarian Han ruler had it changed to a complaint against criticism?[1]

The original final stanza was stanza 37.

NOTES

All sources not included in the selected bibliography
are cited in full in the notes.

INTRODUCTION

1. One aspect of the rejuvenation theme in the *Dao De Jing* involves returning to infancy, about which Joseph Needham has written: "There is no single key to physiological alchemy more important than the idea of retracing one's steps along the road of bodily decay" (*Science and Civilization in China* [Cambridge: Cambridge University Press, 1983], 5:25).

2. This development is found in the *Guanzi,* a late-fourth- to early-third-century B.C. encyclopedia on government compiled in the eastern kingdom of Qi. A similar association of *Dao* and law marks a number of the other texts accompanying the *Dao De Jing* in the Mawangdui tomb. Known collectively as the *Yellow Emperor's Four Classics (Huangdi sijing),* these texts are available in a bilingual edition (Chinese-English) edited by Yu Mingguang: *Huangdi sijing jinzhu jinyi.*

Daoist influence also pervades the writings of the Confucian legalist Xunzi and the legalist Han Feizi. By contrast, the legalist writings of Lord Shang, associated with the central kingdom of Jin, have a sterner, more punitive character, and Daoism plays no role in them.

3. I began this project a half dozen years ago by making a careful study of Gu Li and Zhou Ying's compendious two-volume edition and analysis, *Laozi tong* (A comprehensive Laozi). Though many contemporary scholars may feel that this work has been superseded, it remains a treasure-house of references and thoughtful questions. Among its unusual features is the authors' attempt to re-order radically the sequence of the stanzas. While this effort may have seemed arbitrary or futile, we now know from the Guodian discovery that in the earliest known Laozi the order of the stanzas was indeed altogether different. So in a sense the authors of the *Laozi tong* were correct about the lack of logic in the order of stanzas, the possibility of interpolation within stanzas, and the fact that some stanzas comprise what were originally smaller individual stanzas or even one-line sayings.

4. Yin Zhenhuan, *Boshu Laozi shixi*.

5. For more information on the Fu Yi text and the other received texts, see Rudolf G. Wagner, "The Wang Bi Recension of the *Laozi*" in *Early China* 14 (1989).

6. An English translation of the Mawangdui texts discovered with the *Laozi*, done by Leo S. Chang (Zhang Chun), may be found in Yu Mingguang's critical edition, *Huangdi sijing jinzhu jinyi*, pp. 211–326. Robin D. S. Yates has also translated the Mawangdui documents accompanying the *Laozi*. In the view of the contemporary scholar Bai Xi, the *Huangdi sijing* postdates the *Laozi* but predates the *Guanzi*, the Legalist classic containing texts from the late fourth to early third century B.C. See his *Jixia xue yanjiu*, p. 226.

7. Jingmenshi bowuguan [Museum of the City of Jingmen], *Guodian Chumu zhujian* [Bamboo slips from a Chu tomb at Guodian]. Another edition is Peng Hao, ed., *Guodian Chujian Laozi jiaodu*. An English version is now available: Robert Henricks, *Lao Tzu's* [Laozi's] *Tao Te Ching* [Dao de jing] (New York: Columbia University Press, 2000).

8. This hypothesis has been advanced by Guo Qi in his "Chujian *Laozi* yu *Laozi* gong'an," in *Zhexue yanjiu* 1998.7. A later exponent of this dual attribution is Yin Zhenhuan; see his "Lun Guodian Chumu zhujian *Laozi*," in *Wenxian*, 1999.3, p. 27.

9. Robert Henricks, *Lao-Tzu Te-Tao Ching: A New Translation Based on the Recently Discovered Ma-wang-tui Texts* (New York: Ballantine Books, 1989), p. xvii.

10. The original arrangement of the Fu Yi text, which presumably is contemporaneous if not slightly earlier than the Mawangdui, cannot be determined from the present form of that text.

11. Arguments dating the Heshang gong commentary to the Former Han period may be found in Jin Chunfeng, *Handai sixiangshi* (Beijing: Shehui kexue chubanshe, rev. ed., 1997), pp. 399–411. See also William Boltz, "Lao tzu Tao te ching" in *Early Chinese Texts: A Bibliographical Guide,* ed. Michael Loewe, Early China Special Monograph Series, no. 2 (The Society for the Study of Early China and The Institute of East Asian Studies, University of California, Berkeley, 1993), pp. 273–77.

12. Cited in Xu Kangsheng, *Boshu Laozi*, p. 135.

13. Confucius died in 479 B.C. It has not been established whether the *Analects* were edited and completed at a specific time, say by his followers' followers in the generation 430–400 B.C. (approximately the traditional view), or whether they are a collection of sayings or chapters covering a longer period, from perhaps the mid-fifth century to the mid-third century B.C., as ar-

gued by E. Bruce Brooks and Taeko Brooks in *The Original Analects* (New York: Columbia University Press, 1998). In the present work all references to the *Analects* cite book and chapter and refer to James Legge, trans., *Confucian Analects, The Great Learning, and The Doctrine of the Mean*. Translations of the text may vary from Legge's.

14. For an interesting instance see Herman Hesse's 1921 essay: "Thoughts about China" in *If the War Goes On . . .* (New York: Noonday Press, 1970; repr. 1973), pp. 128–31.

15. These events of the seventh century B.C. are so described in Han Feizi's chapter "Youdu."

16. There is no neat or agreed-upon dividing line between these two periods. Some historians prefer to start the Warring States period at the death of Confucius in 479 B.C. or at the close of the Spring and Autumn Annals a few years later. Others take as the dividing point the year 403 B.C., the year when the Zhou house recognized the three new kingdoms that formed when the older kingdom of Jin broke up. Jin had been the major protector of the Zhou house.

17. In the history of Chinese thought the term *wanwu* (the ten thousand things) becomes prominent from the fourth century on. It is found in the *Mencius,* one hundred times in the *Zhuangzi,* and twenty times in the *Dao De Jing.* However, the term does not appear in the *Zuozhuan,* the *Shijing,* or the *Analects,* which probably date to an earlier time stratum. The term *baiwu* (one hundred things), found once in the *Analects,* seems to be formed by analogy with *baixing,* the one hundred clan names and, by extension, the people in general. *Baiwu* was probably an anticipation of the universal *wanwu.* Perhaps the idea of totalizing all phenomena was first developed by the earliest Daoists.

18. *Zhuangzi,* "Tianxia" ("The World," in Watson's translation). The first to break with Confucian elite subjectivism was Mozi, founder of the Mohist school. Mozi redefined a number of Confucian concepts to shift the balance from the subjective to the objective. He argued that one man should show filial piety to another man's father in hopes of eliciting reciprocal filial piety from the other man toward his own father. He also removed his heaven from the grip of the elite and reconceptualized it as an objective entity above all human claims on its authority. He characterized heaven as a carpenter's measuring tool, thus suggesting its commonness and its accessibility to the common man; the image also suggests its usefulness.

19. The outstanding examples of the new syncretism are, to begin with, the Mawangdui texts found along with the *Laozi,* followed by the *Guanzi,* the

Xunzi, and the *Lüshi chunqiu.* Interestingly, those Mawangdui texts use a number of terms found in the non-Guodian sections of the *Laozi:* the number one *(yi),* receptivity *(xu),* tranquillity or equilibrium *(jing),* and dark virtue *(xuande).* These texts bear clear marks of Laozi's influence.

20. *Analects* 6.21 brings home this point with an elegant metaphor. Confucius likens humanity *(ren)* to mountains and knowledge *(zhi)* to water. Knowledge or expertise is treated by Confucius as a changing and dynamic thing that must shape itself to conform with stationary principles as it flows on. Technology serves morality. Laozi's criticism of expertise is discussed in the body of the present work, e.g., in stanzas 19 and 57.

21. Laozi rejects this ideal in the formula: "Refuse kin-kindness [*ren*], dismiss due service [*yi*], / The folk again will love as child and parent" (stanza 19). Here Laozi rejects not only *ren* but *ren* as an expansion of filial love, which is the central political proposition of the *Analects:* governmental form must be congruent with family structure and values. See comment to stanza 19 for further discussion.

22. Since it is not in the Guodian text, stanza 3 may be hypothetically dated to 375 B.C., in the generation after Mozi's death. According to modern scholar Zhang Songru, "In the history of early Chinese thought Laozi forms the third leg of the tripod with Confucius and Mozi" (*Laozi jiaodu,* p. 439).

23. *Zhanguo ce,* Han 3.

24. *Shijing,* ode 235, "Wenwang." For a translation of the *Shijing,* see Arthur Waley, *The Book of Songs.*

25. *Shujing,* "Kanggao." For the *Shujing,* see Jiang Hao et al., *Jinguwen Shangshu quanyi.*

26. *Shijing,* ode 273, "Shimai."

27. The chapter called "Lun" (Judgments) in the *Huangdi sijing* shows how diversely the term "heaven," freed of its Confucian setting, could be used.

28. One of the crucial differences between the polemical *Dao De Jing* and later Daoist synthesizing texts like the *Wenzi,* the *Huangdi sijing,* and the *Lüshi chunqiu* is that the later works subdivide antiquity *(gu)* into a primal era of formless cosmic forces and a lesser, later era dominated by culture heroes like Fu Xi, Shen Nong, and Huangdi. Thus Laozi's pristine vision was compromised with a mytho-historical phase. See Li Xueqin, "Chu boshu yu Daojia sixiang," in *Daojia wenhua yanjiu,* ed. Chen Guying, 5 (1994), p. 230. Laozi only refers to *gu,* never to specific figures.

29. Mozi's critique of ancestor worship took the form of universalizing the ghosts, making them agents sent by heaven to reward the good and punish evil. Mozi thus turned private gods into public servants. For Confucians, the filial son could appeal for divine ancestral aid, but no one out of the clan could authentically summon them. Mozi's heaven-delegated ghosts no living man has the power to call down. Thus the objective heaven that Mozi sought to create was manifested in this proto-Legalist manner. See Mozi's chapter "Minggui" (Bringing ghosts into the light).

STANZA 1

1. Compare "The number one of the Way was born. / A duad from this monad formed" (stanza 42). Neither stanza 42 nor this opening stanza appear in the Guodian text. However, a cosmogony is offered in *The Great Number One Gives Birth to Water (Taiyi sheng shui)*, another Guodian text that may have been a part of the *Laozi* text group.

2. Guodian text *Yucong* (Collected sayings), item 1. The social virtues—kindness, sense of duty, ritual observance, and knowledge—are what make human beings superior to natural phenomena. For more on the Confucian virtues in the Guodian manuscripts, see Zhang Liwen, "Lüe lun Guodian Chujian de 'ren-yi' sixiang," in *Kongzi yanjiu*, 1999.1.

3. Zhang Songru, *Laozi jiaodu*, p. 10.

4. The possibility of Indian influence is explored in Victor Mair's *Tao Te Ching*. A convenient review of the Chinese antecedents to the *Laozi* may be found in Xu Kangsheng, *Boshu Laozi*, pp. 182–91.

5. The term *zhouxing* in stanza 25, meaning circular movement, parallels this sense of the term *heng*. A number of scholarly articles on the relation of the *Book of Changes* to the *Laozi* may be found in the third volume of a major collection edited by Chen Guying, *Daojia wenhua yanjiu*. Another way to look at the term *chang* is as the antonym of *yao* (abnormal and malign). See *Zuozhuan*, Zhuang 14; and compare stanza 60.

The connection between the number one and *chang* is made in the "Quanyan Xun" section of the *Huainanzi*, p. 692: "If the ruler holds to one, he governs; if he lacks constancy *(chang)*, there will be disorder."

STANZA 2

1. The translation in line 11 interpolates *heng* from the Mawangdui texts, following Chen Guying's *Laozi zhuyi ji pingjie*, p. 66. The words *hengye*, "ever round, and round again," are not in the Guodian text.

2. In line 21 both the Guodian and Mawangdui texts have the word *zhi*, intent, instead of *shi*, rely (translated here as "beholden"). To take this difference into account one would have to shift the subject of the sentence to the wise ruler ("the man of wisdom" in line 12) and translate lines 21–22: "The sage acts without [self-interested] intent; his work completed." This reading is more likely without lines 18–19.

3. *Yucong* (Collected sayings), item 1. Here "nature" is the translation of *xing* not *ziran*.

4. See Yang Shanqun, *Sunzi Pingzhuan* (Guangdong: Nanjing daxue chubanshe, 1992), pp. 200–205. The chapter "Unreal and Real" ("Xushi") contains a list that includes: "strength and weakness, victory and defeat, gain and loss, the few and the many, excess and insufficiency."

According to the "Wu Zixu liezhuan" in the *Shiji*, Sunzi presented a text of his military writings to the ruler of the kingdom of Wu in 512 B.C. Some scholars believe, however, that Sunzi's writings date from the fourth century B.C.

5. A number of *Laozi* stanzas, most of them not in the Guodian find, appear to advocate exploitative dialectics. The theme of *buyan*, not speaking, was turned into advice for the ruler in such Legalist texts as the *Guanzi* and the *Han Feizi*. The ruler was advised to keep his peace in a world of complex contradictions lest by revealing his reaction (or his position) he should cause the ministers to alter information they were bringing to him. See Yin Zhenhuan's notes to stanza 70 in *Boshu Laozi shixi*, p. 204.

STANZA 3

1. See stanza 80 and note 1 for that stanza.

2. Mozi's dates are uncertain. Modern scholar Zhou Jizhi suggests from 485–480 to 415–410 B.C. See his essay on Mozi in volume 1 of the collection of critical biographies of Chinese thinkers: Xin Guanjie and Li Xi, eds., *Zhongguo gudai zhuming zhexuejia pingzhuan* (Shandong province: Qi-Lu shushe, 1980).

3. The first quote is from the chapter in Wang Chong's *Lunheng* titled "Devoting Effort" ("Xiaoli"); the second is *Mencius* 3B.3. Both are cited in Bai Xi, *Jixia xue yanju*, pp. 9–10. In the formulation of Shen Dao (390?–282? B.C.), whose thought forms one of the bridges from Daoism to Legalism, the worthy *(xian)* and the wise *(sheng)* are both to be kept out of government for the sake of the authority of the law. See the section on Shen Dao in the "Tianxia" chapter of the *Zhuangzi*. Laozi praises the wise in both Guodian and non-Guodian sections of the *Laozi* but opposes appointing the worthy.

4. The key phrase of line 16, *wei wuwei* (act on the principle of *wuwei*), is not found in the Mawangdui text.

STANZA 4

1. For a discussion of water in Warring States texts see Sarah Allan, *The Way of Water* (New York: State University of New York Press, 1997) pp. 29–61. Also see the comment to stanza 6, which develops the idea of an underworld river of life. The Guodian essay, found with the *Laozi* portions, called *The Great Number One Gives Birth to Water* treats water as the first creation of the number one, and then makes water the ancestral element for all things.

2. There are various interpretations of line 8. For Wang Bi and Heshang gong, *xiang* simply means "can be imagined as" or "likened to" the ancestor of ancestors. However, *xiang*, image, may be an adjective forming the compound *xiangdi*, imaginable gods; this may refer to the astral signs (*gan* stems) by which the Shang ancestor-kings *(di)* were identified; or the term may refer to the natural imagery (animals, mountains) embodied in the names of such cultural heroes as Yao, Shun, Yu, and Fuxi.

3. For a convincing interpretation of the four phrases, see the excerpt from Ju Zai's *Lun Laozi,* cited in Chen Guying, *Laozi zhuyi ji pingjie.*

STANZA 5

1. See comment to stanza 54.

2. From Su Che's *Laozi jie,* cited in Jiao Hong, *Laozi yi.* Su Che lived from 1039 to 1112. (All Su Che references in this book are from *Laozi jie* as cited in *Laozi yi* by Ming scholar Jiao Hong.)

The straw dog and the clay dragon were used in ceremonies of prayer for rain, according to Chen Yiping, *Huainanzi,* p. 511, fn. 7.

3. *Mozi,* "Tianzhi, shang" (The will of heaven, part 1).

4. *Zhuangzi,* "Tianyun" chapter. The compound for straw dog, *qugou,* is very close in archaic sound to the compound *qurao,* which in the *Mencius* means "chaff and field stubble gathered for fuel."

5. Joseph Needham, *Science and Civilization in China* (Cambridge: Cambridge University Press, 1983), 5:238.

6. *Huainanzi,* "Jingshen" chapter, pp. 317–18. It is possible that Laozi regarded speech as an impediment to the intake of the essence of the Way, hence the emphasis on subjective emptiness (or receptivity, *xu*). Heshang gong titles stanza 5 "The Uses of Emptiness" and in the notes says, "Spare breath energy and minimize speech."

The Heshang gong commentary is founded on a correspondence between the human and cosmic functions. "The Way of Heaven and of man are the same. Heaven and man are in communication, unified by their creative essence and their breath-energy [*jing* and *qi*]." See Na Wei, *Handai Daojia*, p. 255.

7. Su Che's comment owes something to Heshang gong's commentary on the closing lines of this stanza: "Nurture your spiritual powers, spare breath and speak little."

The idea of the zone between heaven and earth being filled with *qi*, an energizing atmosphere that can be drawn inside the body, is also found in the writings of Mencius (see book 2, part 1). In the time of Confucius this zone was often taken to be the domain of ghosts and spirits rather than of a natural (and neutral) ether-like force.

STANZA 6

1. *Huainanzi*, "Dixing" chapter, p. 194.

2. See *Huainanzi*, "Tianwen" chapter, p. 126. For further discussion see John Major, *Heaven and Earth in Early Han Thought* (Albany: State University of New York Press, 1991), pp. 103–4. Also see Sarah Allan, "The Son of Suns," in *The Shape of the Turtle* (New York: State University of New York Press, 1991).

As Allan points out, the myth of the sun's underworld journey probably goes back to the Shang dynasty. A trace of the myth is found in the "Yaodian" of the *Book of Documents (Shujing)*, which says that the sun rises from the Solar Valley. It is probable that the Daoist writers Laozi and Zhuangzi were in touch with those mythic traditions, since they were associated with the kingdom of Chu, and Chu is thought to have retained some of the Shang heritage. In particular, the term for dark, mysterious *(xuan)* that figures in certain *Laozi* stanzas is prominent in bits of lore on the Shang founding ruler preserved in the *Book of Odes (Shijing)*. See ode 303, "Xuanniao" (Dark bird), in which the "dark bird" is a kind of totemic father to the Shang founder.

In Laozi's time the dead were thought to dwell in the Yellow Springs, which were part of the underworld river system. Thus "dark" *(xuan)* could refer to both deep water and the underwater night sky, as well as to the mythic Shang founder.

3. Jiang Xichang, *Laozi jiaogu*, p. 39.

4. *Yuan*, primal, and *tian*, heaven, are linked through the number one, a horizontal line at the top of both graphs.

5. Douglas Wile, *The Chinese Sexual Yoga Classics Including Women's Solo Meditation Texts* (Albany: State University of New York Press, 1992), p. 11.

STANZA 8

1. Chen Guying, *Laozi zhuyi ji pingjie*, pp. 91–92. The *Xiang'er* commentary says that water can accept what is unclean. The idea of the Way as near and intimately involved with human affairs is developed in the "Xinshu, shang" (Mental functions, part 1) chapter of the *Guanzi*: "The Way is near. . . . It resides alongside man but is difficult to find. . . ."

STANZA 10

1. A similar use of *li*, "divided," occurs in the "Mati" (Horses' hooves) chapter of the *Zhuangzi*: *tong hu wu zhi qi de bu li* (when he is one with unknowing, his virtue does not divide). To track the influence of the first two lines on the *Zhuangzi* and the *Guanzi*, see Chen Guying, "Xian-Qin Daojia yanjiu de xin fangxiang," in *Daojia wenhua yanjiu* 6 (1995), pp. 31–32.

Li is also a military term, where it means division or disintegration. The *Sunzi Bingfa* says, "If the enemy enjoys solidarity, then create divisions among them." See the opening chapter, "Ji" (General plans). For a translation see Sun-tzu, *The Art of War*, trans. Ralph Sawyer (Barnes and Noble for Westview Press, 1994).

2. For a discussion of *po*, "new-moon soul," and further references see David W. Pankenier, "The Metempsychosis in the Moon," *The Museum of Far Eastern Antiquities*, Bulletin 58 (1986), pp. 149–55. It is uncertain that the spectrum of *yin-yang* references suggested by commentators was known to the author of stanza 10. The terms *yin* and *yang* occur only once in the *Laozi*, in non-Guodian stanza 42.

3. The term *qi* (life force, physical vitality, breath energy) occurs three times in the *Laozi*, and only once in the Guodian text. It has been suggested that use of the term *qi* in this basic physical sense in the *Huangdi sijing* means that this text group is closer in time to the *Laozi*. In contrast, the four *Guanzi* chapters probably postdate both because they make a compound of the terms *jing* and *qi*, which are used in a philosophical more than a physiological sense. See Wang Bo, "*Huangdi sijing* he *Guanzi* sipian" in *Daojia wenhua yanjiu*, ed. Chen Guying, no. 1.

For further discussion see Chen Guying's essay on the central role of Daoist thought in the pre-Qin period, "Daojia zai xian-Qin zhexueshih shang de zhugan diwei," in *Daojia wenhua yanjiu*, no. 10, pp. 43–45.

4. Chen Guying, *Laozi zhuyi ji pingjie*, pp. 98–99. In *Mencius* the mind of an infant *(chizi zhi xin)* is used to suggest innocence prior to the development

of the emotions. But Mencius speaks of the infant developing its natural potential, not maintaining its original state.

STANZA 11

1. See the chapter "Zhushu xun" (Ruler's craft), p. 395, in the *Huainanzi* and the interpretation by Gao You. The wheel spokes image is also found in the chapter "Dafen" (Great hierarchy) of the Mawangdui text *Jingfa* (*Huangdi sijing*, pp. 32–33).

STANZA 12

1. Burton Watson, *Mo Tzu*.

2. "Liufen" in *Jingfa*, *Huangdi sijing*, p. 35. It is characteristic of this Mawangdui text to reformulate Laozi's stern critique of rulers, requiring merely that they be justified by and answerable to law and not arbitrarily govern at their own discretion. The *Jingfa* tries to find a middle way between the abstinence Laozi demands and the lusts that the powerful will seek to indulge. As the character of the ruler becomes less important, law becomes more so. Law in the *Jingfa* is made transcendent and objective as a creation of the Way. Thus legalism puts the Way to use as a legitimator of law.

STANZA 13

1. "Dafen," in *Jing fa*, *Huangdi sijing*, p. 37.

2. Gu Li and Zhou Ying, *Laozi tong*, 1:438.

STANZA 14

1. Wang Li, *Laozi yanjiu*, p. 11. See also Na Wei, *Handai Daojia*, p. 94.

2. *Huainanzi*, "Yuan Dao xun," p. 21.

STANZA 15

1. For an extended discussion of the philological problems in this stanza (based on the Mawangdui version) see William G. Boltz, "Manuscripts with Transmitted Counterparts," in *New Sources of Early Chinese History*, ed. Edward Shaughnessy (Berkeley: Society for the Study of Early China and the Institute of East Asian Studies, University of California, 1997).

2. *Cheng* is the third of the four texts other than the *Laozi* discovered at Mawangdui. See Yu Mingguang, *Huangdi sijing*. In the list of *yin-yang* phenomena we find "the king is *yang*, his ministers *yin*; . . . large kingdoms are *yang*, small ones *yin*."

STANZA 16

1. The Guodian text's *zhong* (center, within, inner state) in the place of *jing* (stability, quiet) suggests a more Confucian tone to line 2. *Jing* is a staple term of Zhuangzi Daoism.

2. The Guodian text has "await" *(xu)* in the place of "contemplate" *(guan)* in line 4.

3. The Guodian text includes only the first six lines of this stanza (for the word "root" [*gen*] see comment and note 2 to stanza 6):

1   Achieving receptivity, [requires] constancy
2   Guarding one's inner life, perseverance
3   Once the ten thousand have come forth,
4   [I] await their return to whence they began
5   The Way of heaven goes round and round
6   Each and every returns to the root.

Guo Qi regards the Guodian text as superior to all later ones. See his "Chu-jian 'Laozi' yu Laozi gong'an," in *Guodian Chujian yanjiu*, ed. Jiang Kuanghui, Zhongguo zhexue, no. 20.

4. See *Guanzi*, "Xinshu, shang."

STANZA 17

1. Cited in Wei Qipeng, "Fan Li ji qi Tiandao guan," in *Daojia wenhua yanjiu* 6 (1995), p. 96.

STANZA 18

1. *Zhong*, "loyal," is not found in the Mawangdui or Guodian texts. The latter has *zheng* (upright, correcting), and the former has *zhen* (of integrity, pure, worthy of performing divination). *Zheng* and *zhen* sometimes function as synonyms.

2. Gu Li and Zhou Ying, *Laozi tong*, 1:138.

STANZA 19

1. Comment by Lü Jifu, cited in Jiao Hong, *Laozi yi*.

2. From Yang Xingshun's *Zhongguo gudai zhexuejia Laozi jiqi xueshuo*, cited in Chen Guying, *Laozi zhuyi ji pingjie*.

3. The Guodian text of this stanza differs significantly, however, since line 3's phrase "Refuse kin-kindness, dismiss due service" seems to read: "Refuse false practices and treacherous schemes." Moreover, the dramatic open-

ing line, "Refuse the wise, dismiss the intellects," reads: "Refuse the wise, dismiss cunning argument." The uncertain, pivotal lines 7 and 8 connect the bold injunctions of lines 1–6 to the positive homily in lines 9 and 10. Lines 7 and 8 also differ in the Guodian text. Instead of the word "as text" we find the word "distinctions/arguments." The point seems to be that the three rejections in lines 1–6 are inadequate unless accompanied by a simplified economic lifestyle on the part of those who rule. The Guodian lines 7 and 8 seem to say, "These three [shalt-nots] do not yet suffice / Some things [lines 1–6?] can be decreed [forbidden?]; some [the final lines?] require commitment."

STANZA 20

1. These four lines are found in the Guodian text, where they are followed by stanza 13. The remainder of this stanza, a sort of self-portrait, is not there. This bears out the speculation of Yin Zhenhuan ("Huifu Laozi de ben-lai mianmu," *Wenxian*, 1992.3, p. 75) that the first four lines formed a separate stanza. Their theme is close to that of the opening of stanza 2—opposites can easily turn into one another—with an additional warning about reversals of political fortune.

2. According to Wang Bi's note, line 5 describes Laozi "sighing at his separation from ordinary life." Modern scholar Gao Heng places this line between lines 9 and 10.

Following the cue of the Guodian text, which contains only the first four lines of this stanza, line 5 would be the first line of another stanza—not in the Guodian text—comprising the remaining lines. However, the connection of line 5 to the rest of the stanza is uncertain.

3. Both the Heshang gong and the Wang Bi commentaries interpret the *xi-xi* descriptive compound in line 6 to mean "high in spirits." This stanza carries a faint echo of Song Keng's philosophy of remaining detached from custom (*bu lei yu su*).

4. "Without guile" in line 15 is the translation for *wo yuren zhi xin* (my simpleton heart). The word *yu* in the sense of foolish or simple should be understood in connection with the word *pu*, simplicity, implying lack of desire. See the discussion of this stanza by Wang Lijia "Lun Laozi de 'pu' zhi si-xiang," in *Guanzi xuekan* (1998.3), pp. 78–79.

5. This line seems to go better in stanza 15 (where it appears as lines 10–11) than in stanza 20, despite the fact that it occurs here in the main received texts. In the Mawangdui texts the line reads: "How gloomy like the sea; how restless, with nowhere to rest."

6. For an English translation of Qu Yuan's poetry see David Hawkes, *The Songs of the South*. Some scholars have dated the *Laozi* between Qu Yuan's work and the *Shijing* as a philosophical poem that shares themes and styles with both. The phonological scholar William H. Baxter makes a similar judgment based on the rhyming patterns in the three texts. See his "Situating the Language of the *Laozi*," in *Lao-Tzu and the Tao-te-ching*, ed. Livia Kohn and Michael LaFargue.

7. Jiao Hong, *Laozi yi*.

8. *Huangdi sijing, Jingfa*, "Junzheng." The words *zi* and *min* ("sons" and "people") may be taken together as a rhetorical division of the phrase *zimin*, meaning the people as subjects (sons).

STANZA 21

1. In Warring States texts the word *xin*, trust, often interchanges with *shen*, extend; and *shen* in the sense of "extend" is a homophone of and basic definition for *shen* in the sense of "body." The common phrase *youshen* means "to be pregnant." "A quickening," then, could replace "a thing to trust," or as a pun widen the meaning of line 9.

In line 8, the word *jing*, "germ of life," also refers to both semen and the fluid produced by the female when sexually aroused. The Mawangdui versions have *qing*, essential characteristics, not *jing*. The Zhuangzi chapter "Xu Wugui" speaks of "being attuned to the *qing* of heaven and earth." Despite variations in the secondary or radical element, the core meaning of both *jing* and *qing* is anchored in the phonetic, which means life force, growing thing. More abstractly, perhaps, *tiandi zhi qing* can be translated "living essence of nature," i.e., heaven and earth.

2. For more detail on this hypothesis, see Gu Li and Zhou Ying, *Laozi tong*, 1:41; Gu Li follows Jiang's suggestion. Though there are a few Mohist craftsman metaphors for the Way in the *Laozi*, generally maternal metaphors for the creation process dominate the *Laozi*.

3. The common phrase *cong-rong* is split (and reversed: *rong-cong*) to end the first couplet. The words mean "unhurried, unforced, acceptance of the natural progress of things." Virtue follows the Way as if it were an obedient wife or vassal, but without compulsion.

STANZA 22

1. The key terms of line 1, *qu* and *quan* (bent and whole, translated here as "bend" and "to not break"), occur in the "Tianxia" chapter of *Zhuangzi*:

"All men seek good fortune; I alone bend to remain whole. This means doing whatever is necessary to avoid the wrath of heaven"—that is, to survive.

2. The present translation follows Gu Li's emendation, which takes the first line of stanza 23 (*xi yan zi ran*) as the last of stanza 22. The rather elliptical phrase suggests that a minimum of speech (and thus also a minimum of naming and action) allows things to take their natural course. This line, however, may simply be a single-line stanza. Yin Zhenhuan interprets it as a single stanza that means "Speak as little as possible about the so-ness of things."

3. The section of stanza 22 composed of lines 6–16 seems thematically linked to stanza 24, while stanza 23 may belong elsewhere. The Mawangdui editor places 24 just before 22, acknowledging the affinity of the two stanzas.

4. Wei Yuan, *Laozi benyi*. Wei Yuan lived from 1794 to 1854.

5. *Huangdi sijing, Shiliu jing,* "Xingzheng." For the anti-statist Zhuangzi, oneness is not a means to power or control over the ten thousand or the world below the sky, but rather the means to merge or unite with the ten thousand.

STANZA 24

1. In the Mawangdui text stanza 24 is in place of stanza 22 and vice versa.

STANZA 25

1. The Guodian text has all lines of this stanza except line 5. According to Cui Renyi, a scholar of the Guodian texts, the first line reads *you jiang hun cheng* (what is beginning to take inchoate form). See his *Jingmen Guodian Chujian Laozi yanjiu,* p. 41. At the end of line 2 in the Guodian text a binom appears: *dui-mu.* Unattested elsewhere, perhaps the graphs should be read *dun-mo* (solid, profound, silent). In Mawangdui text the binom is *xiao-liao* (desolate-remote), and in the received text, *ji-liao* (isolated-remote). Line 3 of this translation is an attempt to render the binom into English.

2. Line 5 fits well with the idea of a vast cyclical motion that the Way imposes upon all it creates. However, the line is not found in either the Guodian or Mawangdui texts. "Fail" is the translation of *dai,* which literally means abort. A parallel line in the *Daoyuan* of the *Huangdi sijing* says that the Way "stands alone and forms no pair." This phrase, "no pair" *(buou),* could refer to the Way's single state or to the phrase "match the high ancestors" *(pei shangdi)* in the ode "Wenwang." The word *pei* refers to the matching or correlating of a sovereign with the ancestors or with heaven. *Pei* also means to marry.

In the Guodian manuscript, in place of the last word of the preceding line, *gai*, change, is a homophone, *gai* meaning "come to an end, have a limit."

3. In line 16, "man" replaces "kings" *(wang)* in the Guodian and Mawang-dui manuscripts. Embedded in the ancient graph for "king" is the graph for "man," the vertical line dividing into two legs in the lower half: *wang* means leader, or he who walks ahead. The shift from "king" to "man" may have been influenced by a statement Zengzi attributes to Confucius: "Born of heaven, nourished by earth, man is greatest." See Dai De's *Da Dai Liji,* "Zengzi daxiao."

4. *Gongyang zhuan.* Yingong 1.

5. The final words in the Chinese, *ziran*, here translated as "self-momentum" (and as "nature" by Chan, "naturally so" by Mair, "self-So" by Waley) may also mean "the way things are," "all as it is given." A less static translation—conveying motion rather than being—seems preferable. The Heshang gong commentary says that "by its very nature the Way is self-becoming *(ziran);* it does not 'comply with' anything." The shift from a transcendent to an immanent Way is seen in this stanza.

STANZA 26

1. See the chapter in Sunzi's *Art of War* entitled "Armies in Conflict" ("Junzheng"). The Mawangdui texts as well as the *Han Feizi* and the *Xiang'er* text have *junzi* in line 3, while the Heshang gong and Wang Bi editions have *shengren.*

2. *Han Feizi*, "Yu Lao." Sunzi says that "without its stockage wagons an army is doomed." See Gu Li and Zhou Ying, *Laozi tong,* 1:350–55.

STANZA 27

1. Compare the use of *jie,* to tie a knot, in line 6 with *jie* in the Guodian text *Zhongxin zhi dao* (The Way of loyalty and dependability): "Complete dependability is like the seasons, which complete their cycles needing no binding agreement *(jie)."*

2. "Far-reaching insight" is the translation of *ximing.* The meaning of *xi,* translated here as "far-reaching," is not settled. The Mawangdui text A has *shen* ("extend" plus the radical for heart-mind) instead of *xi* ("pursue," a homophone for "practiced"). Yin Zhenhuan interprets *shen* according to the dictionary definition "anxiety" and interprets *shenming* in line 12 to mean "the wisdom that comes from experience of troubles" ("Boshu *Laozi* hanyi butong de wenju" in *Daojia wenhua yanjiu,* no. 10, p. 150). In the late Warring

States period the word *shen* may not have been very firmly bonded with its radical, so here it may mean divine, yielding the common phrase *shenming* (godlike or uncanny insight), "extended mentally," "far-reaching."

3. Lines 13 and 14 are translated here following the Mawangdui text. The modern texts have what seems to be an extra negative, yielding the meaning: "The expert instructs the *un*fit / The unfit provides the expert with subjects."

STANZA 28

1. A number of commentators have suspected that the last four lines, 19–22, are a later interpolation that has become integrated into the stanza.

2. Many scholars have expressed doubt about the integrity of the text for this stanza. Based on citations in the chapter "Tianxia" in *Zhuangzi*, Zhang Songru has reconstructed what he believes to be the original text. See his comment in *Laozi jiaodu*, pp. 173–77.

STANZA 29

1. The verb in line 1, *qu* (seize, capture), is a common military term.

Many scholars have suggested a relationship, if not a mixing up of lines, between this stanza and stanza 64. However, this stanza is not found in the Guodian manuscript, while stanza 64 is. On the other hand, the opening chapter of the Mawangdui document "Daofa" of the *Jingfa* says, "He who seizes hold of the Way regards the world as follows: nothing seizing, nothing settled on, nothing leading, nothing for himself." The term *wusi*, "nothing for self," is also used in the "Daofa" as a prerequisite for impartial, law-based government. One possible translation for "Daofa" is "Law based on the Way."

The "Daofa" seems to develop the theme of this stanza; if it was composed around the mid-fourth century B.C., this could date this stanza back to the first generation of the fourth century.

2. See *Zuozhuan*, Xuangong 3, which dates the incident to 605 B.C.

STANZA 30

1. Line 4 is found in the Mawangdui text but not the Guodian text. According to Yin Zhenhuan, the Mawangdui editor was reinforcing the antiwar theme of the *Laozi* by illustrating the hardship war imposes on farming communities. See his "Lun 'Guodian Chumu zhujian Laozi'" in *Wenxian* 1999.3, p. 20.

Line 5 is not found in either the Mawangdui or the Guodian texts; it was apparently added later, again to reinforce the antiwar theme.

2. This stanza appears in the Guodian manuscript; however, lines 3–5 and 12–14 are not included. The Guodian text ends with what, on the other hand, seems to be an incomplete rendering of line 3. Lines 12–14 seem to fit better at the end of the preceding stanza, 29, than at the end of this one.

3. Zhang Songru, *Laozi jiaodu*, pp. 183–85. The Wang Zhen text, together with the *Laozi*, has been translated by Ralph Sawyer in *The Tao of Peace* (Boston and London: Shambhala, 1999).

STANZA 31

1. Heshang gong interprets line 9 to mean "with no ambition to seize territory or capture treasure." For "unstirred" the Guodian and Mawangdui B texts have an unfamiliar binom, *xian-long,* that has not been satisfactorily interpreted.

2. *Zhongyong* (section 10). Known as the "Doctrine of the Mean," the *Zhongyong* is probably a post-Laozi text. However a number of its formulations are found in some of the Guodian texts.

The "Banfa Jie" chapter of the *Guanzi* links the left with spring and the renewal of life, and the right with autumn and death. The terms *wen* and *wu* (civil and military) are also associated in this passage with left and right, respectively.

For more on left and right, see "Laozi and Guanzi" by Guzhong Xinyi, an article translated from the Japanese in *Guanzi xuekan* 1994.2, p. 14.

3. See Sun Bin's *Art of War,* the section "Weiwang Wen" or "Questions of King Wei [of Qi]."

STANZA 32

1. The opposition between *ming* (name, fame) and *Dao* is expressed in the "Quanyan" section of the *Huainanzi:* "Name and the Way do not form a pair [like sun and moon]. When men gain name, then the Way is put aside; when the Way conquers things human, then name and fame cease to matter" (p. 689).

However, it is possible to parse line 1 after *wu* (the negative in "unnamed") and take *ming,* name, as the start of the next sentence. This would yield for the first three lines: "The Way is constantly negating. / Call it unhewn rawness. / No king in the realm can make the Way serve him."

2. In the Guodian text lines 2–3 read: "A servant, a wife, whom none can compel to serve." Compare the Mawangdui text *Daoyuan,* which says, "The Way stands alone, with no spouse, but nothing can compel her to serve." This language reinforces the theme of *Dao* as a female power that cannot be

dominated. The *Xiang'er* note to this stanza captures the point regarding gender: "The Way is low and humble and as the mother of the realm cannot be made to serve."

3. Lines 8–10 are interpreted by Gao Heng: "To begin with, the name *Dao* was fashioned; and after that, the lords and kings could know it, and knowing it, avoid danger." For the argument see his *Laozi zhenggu*. More commonly, *ming*, "names," is taken negatively to mean trappings of status and the loss of an original social unity based on primitive economic equity.

4. The formlessness *(wuxing)* of water *(shui)* in the closing line echoes the shapelessness of unhewn rawness *(pu)* in the second line. Nothing can bend the formless or the shapeless to its purposes. The following passage from "Xinshu" (Mental functions) may shed some light on this stanza: "The Way of Heaven is void in its formlessness. Void, it never becomes depleted; formless, nothing can make it submit to exploitation. Thus it circulates through the ten thousand without itself undergoing change" (*Guanzi*, "Xinshu, shang").

5. The last line of stanza 28 says that "fine cutters never harm the stone." In stanza 19 occurs the famous phrase *baopu*, "embrace rawness" or "embrace simplicity" (translated there as "humble habits"), which later became the title of a Daoist compilation of hygienic regimens, alchemical treatises, and philosophical counsels.

6. Toward the last decades of the fourth century B.C. *di*, an ancient term for ruler, reappeared. In the *Guanzi*, for example, which was an important Qi kingdom text heavily influenced by Laozi, the words *di*, emperor, and *tianzi*, son of heaven, are used to designate the supreme ruler. In the chapter "Chengma" the *di* figure is singled out as the highest for his practice of *wuwei*, under-action. For further discussion see Hu Jiacong, *Guanzi xintan*. The terms *tianzi*, *di*, and *ba* (hegemon) became widely used in the late fourth century; they are found in the *Mencius* as well, which was associated with Qi. Their absence in any *Laozi* text suggests an earlier period for the *Laozi* as well as a different venue, presumably the kingdom of Chu.

STANZA 33

1. Line 6 is interpreted in the light of stanza 36 and the phrase in stanza 52: "Real strength keeps to the gentle side."

STANZA 34

1. The Mawangdui texts do not include lines 3–4 of this stanza. The translation of *ci* as shirk is uncertain. For a discussion of the problems see

Alan K. L. Chan, *Two Visions of the Way: A Study of the Wang Pi and Ho-shang Kung Commentaries on the Lao-Tzu* (Albany: State University of New York Press, 1991), pp. 110–11.

2. This stanza is not found in the Guodian manuscript. In the Mawangdui texts lines 3 and 9 are identical to each other, perhaps a scribal error. Lines 4–5 as translated here are found in the received texts.

STANZA 36

1. Jiang Xichang, *Laozi jiaogu;* and Gao Heng, *Chongding Laozi zhenggu.*
2. Gu Li and Zhou Ying, *Laozi tong,* 1:158.
3. Chen Guying, *Laozi zhuyi ji pingjie,* p. 206.

STANZA 37

1. There is no word for "we" in the Guodian text, so the subject of the verb "humble" in line 6 would be the "lords and kings" who conform to the Way (line 3).

2. There is a phonetic connection between *wei,* action, translated as "pursuing no end" in line 2, and *hua* in line 4, "turn in trust." The two words sounded similar: **ngua,* with a broad *a*-rhyme and a *gw-* or *ngw-* initial. Possibly the two constitute a word cline with *hua* in the sense of change, convert—referring to the result of a positive or negative action *(wei),* like the fourth principal part of a Latin verb. The link between the two words is strengthened by the fact that in the Guodian and Mawangdui A texts *hua* in stanza 37 is written with the graph for *wei* enlarged by the heart element. "Transform" seems both too strong and too unclear for *hua.* The *Guanzi* chapter "Qifa" (Seven laws) defines *hua* as follows: "It means gradual, smooth, accommodating, prolonged, conforming, and habitual." The implication of the term is that the ruler's influence becomes as irresistible as a natural force.

3. It is almost certain that *chang* is a synonym for the original *heng* (which had to be avoided by the Mawangdui scribes, since it was the name of Emperor Wen of the Han). The sense of recurring process for *heng* is suggested by *Shijing* ode 166, "Tianbao," whose sixth stanza opens with the line "Like the reliable old *(heng)* moon." See also the comment to stanza 1.

4. The contemporary scholar Yin Zhenhuan has addressed this stanza in two important articles. He sees the key phrase in line 2, "Pursuing no end leaves nothing not done" *(wuwei er wu buwei),* as unnecessary hyperbole, an omnipotence that no political authority can or should aspire to. Accordingly, Yin prefers the more modest and practicable Mawangdui language:

1 The Way is ever nameless
2 If lords and kings could keep to this
3 The ten thousand will turn to them in trust
4 If desires nonetheless arise
5 We shall contain them with the simplicity of no-naming
6 And having done so
7 They [lords and kings] shall never know disgrace
8 Not knowing disgrace they will have peace and content
9 And heaven and earth will come to right order of themselves.

This version strikes a note of humility rather than omnipotence. The rulers eschew name and thus avoid disgrace (*ru;* instead of *yu*, desire). For comparison, a translation of the Guodian version is provided here. Note the variations in the closing line:

1 The Way pursues no end;
2 Let lords and kings abide by this
3 And all will turn to them in trust
4 And if desire should yet arise
5 Let them suppress it with the stark simplicity of no-names.
6 And they shall know when to be satisfied.
7 And restrained by knowing when to be satisfied;
8 The ten thousand will then come to order of themselves.

The Mawangdui may be a better reading, but it is not necessarily the earliest. The Guodian text has "The Way pursues no end." The hyperbolic "nothing not done" is not found here, but it is found in the Guodian equivalent of stanza 48. For Yin's discussion, see "Zai lun 'Mawangdui Hanmu boshu Laozi'" in *Wenxian* 1995.

In another article Yin argues that stanza 37, as the final stanza of the whole text, accents the theme of no-naming *(wuming)*, which is more important (if occurring less frequently) than the theme of under-action *(wuwei)*. In Yin's view, under-action is realized through not naming. See his "Laozi de wu ming sixiang" in the *Fudan xuebao, she-ke ban* 1992.2.

5. For example, "It is the natural temperament of all men to go for what benefits them and avoid what harms them. . . . They will go without being pushed and come without being led; without [troublesome] injunctions or [unwanted] disturbance the people will enrich themselves" (*Guanzi*, "Jin-zang" [Restricting accumulation]). The setting for this passage is the description of a kingdom with highly developed technical, economic, and military resources—the antithesis of Laozi's ideal community.

6. See Bai Xi, *Jixia xue yanjiu,* pp. 92–96.

1. There are strong arguments for translating lines 5–6: "High Virtue pursues no end / And leaves no end ungained." See Miao Ming-chun, "Laozi 'wu wei er wu buwei' shuo xin zheng," in *Guodian Chujian yanjiu*, ed. Jiang Kuanghui, Zhongguo zhexue, no. 20, pp. 154–55.

2. Lines 7–8 break the pattern of lines 5–13; this contested line does not appear in the Mawangdui texts. An extended discussion of the various textual choices for lines 1–12 may be found in Chen Guying, *Laozi zhuyi ji pingjie*, pp. 213–14. Most scholars take lines 1–4 to mean that high virtue negates itself and thus has virtue; low virtue never negates itself and thus lacks virtue. *De* as a verb often means to benefit or perform a favor for someone, which then obliges them.

3. Yin Zhenhuan's reading of lines 14–15 is singular though intriguing: the performers of ritual persevere in the ritual even though they receive no response (*Boshu Laozi shixi*, p. 37). This could refer to the loss of public enthusiasm for hereditary ritual. "Ritual is an exercise in mutual hypocrisy," according to the "Zhibeiyou" chapter ("Knowledge Wandered North" in Watson's translation) of the *Zhuangzi*. "Zhibeiyou" cites lines 16–25 of this stanza.

4. Lines 26–27 say that terms mentioned in the preceding lines—virtue, kindness, service, and ritual—decorate the Way with flowers, falsifying it. This severe stricture against ritual contrasts with the *Guanzi*'s qualified acceptance of ritual.

5. The five stages of devolution—the Way, virtue, human kindness, honorable service, and ritual *(Dao, de, ren, yi, li)*—may mimic and even mock devolution theories of the five elements.

6. Han Feizi in his chapter "Jie Lao" ("Explaining Laozi") treats the term *qianshi* (translated in line 26 as "all that has been learned") as "preconception" or "prejudice." Almost all commentators follow Han Feizi. Translators usually choose "foreknowledge," but what this has to do with this stanza remains unexplained. It seems rather to refer to previously inculcated values. A passage from Zhuangzi's "Zhibeiyou" reads: "Ritual is the bedecking of the Way and the source of social disorder. Thus it was said, 'Pursue the Way by unlearning day by day.'" This interesting Zhuangzi passage suggests that the puzzling words *qianshi* may not belong in the text at all; it also shows that two *Laozi* references—to this stanza and to stanza 48—were cited as authority and related to one another by the author of the "Zhibeiyou."

7. *Liji*, "Quli, shang."

STANZA 39

1. The Mawangdui text reads *zheng* (straighten, rectify), not *zhen* (to divine, integrity of the diviner), translated here as "tell their fate." Rectification, a term more political than religious, is the primary responsibility of the ruler in the *Analects*. However, in the Guodian text, in place of *zhen*, to divine, we find the verb *zhen*, to control politically and militarily. That would mean that the kings and lords "rule their state" instead of "tell their fate."

2. Stanza 38 is not included in the Guodian text; the second part of stanza 39 is. In Confucian texts *yue*, music, is typically found in combination with *li*, ritual. The sequence is *li yue*, with ritual first, suggesting discipline and social hierarchy, and then music, suggesting the common community and the sublimation of ritual distinctions in a common harmony.

3. "Embrace the Way and hold tight to standards, and all under heaven can be unified" (Mawangdui text *Daoyuan*). In the Huang-Lao texts of the state of Qi (and in the *Mencius* as well) unification of the empire *(tianxia)* emerges as the long-range ideal goal of political action. The *Laozi* does not speak of unifying the empire, simply of straightening it out. This is either because it predates the emergence of unification as an issue or because it opposes unification. Compare the passage in the *Zhuangzi*: "Those of old who nurtured the world below had no desire and the world was content, did not act and all things were transformed, remained tranquil and the people were stable and orderly" ("Tiandi" [Heaven and earth]).

4. Yan Zun, *Laozi zhigui*, p. 11.

5. *Analects* 1.15. For a discussion of the symbolism of jade and bronze in music-making, see Scott Cook, "Consummate Artistry and Moral Virtuosity: The 'Wu xing' Essay and Its Aesthetic Implications," in *Chinese Literature: Essays, Articles, Reviews* 22 (2000), p. 129.

6. The first complete dictionary, *Shuowen jiezi* (ca. A.D. 100) pairs *tian* and *yuan* under the element *yi*, one. In words like *dan*, dawn, and *li*, stand, the horizontal represents the ground or earth; in *tian* and *yuan* it represents heaven.

7. In an article on the number one, Yin calls attention to the link between *yi* and *ben* (foundation) in the "Wuxing" (Five agents) section of the *Guanzi*. *Ben* typically refers to agriculture as the foundation of the economy and the political order, and ritual as well. Yin Zhenhuan ties this stanza to stanza 50 in his article, "*Laozi Guanzi de yi jiqi fazhan*," *Guanzi xuekan* 1991.3, pp. 16–22.

8. For discussion of *taiyi* and its relation to *Dao*, see Rao Zongyi, "Boshu 'xi ci zhuan' da heng shuo," in *Daojia wenhua yanjiu*, ed. Chen Guying, 3 (1993). For a discussion of *yi*, one, in the *Laozi* and the *Guanzi*, see Yin Zhenhuan, "*Laozi Guanzi de yi jiqi fazhan*," *Guanzi xuekan* 1991.3.

For Confucius's use of the number one, see *Analects* 4.15: "My Way is organized around one single [principle]." This is explained as referring to ethical practices, loyalty, and reciprocity—a philosophical unity rather than a metaphysical power.

STANZA 40

1. This stanza is identical in the Guodian text, except that the last line may lack the *you* that begins line 4. That would make the ten thousand the offspring of what is and what is not as a pair. The present text, on the other hand, describes the ten thousand as descended from what is, and what is as descended from what is not.

2. In stanza 11 the function of the wheel depends on the complementary use of the "existing" spokes and the "nonexisting" hub in which the axle turns. In stanza 25 the term *fan* (contra-motion, reversal) first appears: after *Dao* has "reached far" it begins to turn back. Jiang Xichang takes "reaching far" *(yuan)* to refer to the excesses and complications of society. Disorder occurs when things have departed too far from their simple foundations. What is and what is not have a natural balance that should be maintained.

3. *Guanzi*, "Renfa" (Giving authority to law) is the chapter title. That law is compatible with government by ruler and vassal is shown in the chapter titled "Junchen" (Rulers and vassals), which draws on the Confucian concept of ritual to preserve political distinctions in a Daoist-Legalist context. (See Bai Xi, *Jixia xue yanjiu*, pp. 230–31.)

4. Stanza 42 is not found in the Guodian text; instead, stanza 40 precedes stanza 9 and follows stanza 44.

STANZA 41

1. This reading is the conventional interpretation; the meaning of line 9 remains unsolved. Yin Zhenhuan suggests: "Those who do harm to the Way seem to foster it." See *Boshu Laozi shixi*, pp. 52–53.

2. The Mawangdui text reads *bao* (cherish, praise) in place of *yin* (unknown, concealed). (In the *Mencius*, *yin* means sympathize.) So the Mawangdui line may mean "The Way cherishes all without name."

3. The meaning of line 21 is echoed in stanza 64: "How often the people,

assuming a task, / Ruin it at the verge of success?" Finishing well is rare, starting well is not.

4. See *Zhuangzi*, "Tianxia."

5. Gu Li and Zhou Ying, *Laozi tong*, 1:611.

STANZA 42

1. The first eight lines of this stanza are probably the sequel to stanza 40, lines 3–4. The remainder of the stanza, lines 9–18, seem to be a separate stanza.

2. *Huangdi sijing*, pp. 146–47.

STANZA 43

1. *Huangdi sijing*, p. 149.

STANZA 44

1. Compare stanza 13, which advocates freeing the self of name and status.

2. This stanza is found virtually word for word in the Guodian text. Laozi does not often mention economic production as a social activity. In contrast, the *Huangdi sijing* refers to production on several occasions (in *Jingfa* and *Cheng,* for example), developing economic thought while retaining the Way as the principal referent.

STANZA 45

1. Zhang Zhenze, *Sun Bin bingfa jiaoli,* p. 147. Compare the section entitled "Shundao" in the Mawangdui text *Shiliu jing:* "In war show unwillingness to fight, display your inability."

2. The name of the well-known philosophical school called Qingtan, or "Pure Conversation," derives from these lines.

3. Jiao Hong, *Laozi yi.* Lines 9–12 may form a separate stanza.

STANZA 46

1. In line 5 the Guodian text has *shenyu,* extreme desire, rather than *keyu,* sanctioned desire. Some texts have lines 6 and 7 but lack line 5; however, the Guodian has all three.

STANZA 47

1. If the word *ming* in line 7 is not "name" but "vision," as the Han Feizi "Yu Lao" chapter has it, then the meaning would be to perceive without seeing.

2. The metaphor of staying safely behind a closed door is found in Sunzi's *Art of War* in the chapter titled "Jiudi" (Nine terrains). Sunzi uses "door" as a military metaphor: "Once the enemy opens his door, act as swiftly as a racing hare, before the enemy has time to defend himself."

3. The *Guanzi* attributes this statement to Song Keng, who predated Mencius and wrote in the Daoist tradition. The language of his formulation suggests that he drew his metaphor from Laozi's "door" and "window."

4. The relevant *Guanzi* chapters on the elements and functioning of the mind are "Neiye" (Internal tasks), "Baixin" (Explaining the mind), and "Xinshu" (Mental functions).

STANZA 48

1. The last four lines, somewhat reminiscent of a surviving formula of the mid-fourth century B.C. legalist Shen Buhai, give the stanza a turn in the direction of cunning statecraft. Shen Buhai had written that "the ruler must conceal his methods within [an appearance of] no-action" and "display to the world his non-pursuit of an end" (cited in Yang Kuan, *Zhanguoshi*, rev. ed., [Shanghai: Shanghai renmin chubanshe, 1998], p. 198).

2. Guo Qi, "Chujian *Laozi* yu Laozi gong'an," in *Guodian Chujian yanjiu*, ed. Jiang Kuanghui, Zhongguo zhexue, no. 20, pp. 118–47.

STANZA 49

1. "Success in governing lies in conforming to the people's mind" (*Guanzi*, "Mumin"). A short list of similar relevant quotations may be found in Yu Zhenhuan, *Boshu Laozi shixi*, p. 91.

Baixing, one hundred surnames, in line 2 is often translated as if it were *laobaixing*, the common people. Since the non-Guodian portions of the text may be early-to-mid fourth century B.C. or earlier, this is the more likely translation. This is also the interpretation preferred by scholars who see Laozi as a spokesman for the exploited or for the peasantry. (See for instance Zhan Jianfeng, *Laozi qiren qishu ji qidao lun* [Changsha: Hubei renmin chubanshe, 1982], pp. 469–70.)

2. There are varying interpretations of this stanza. A different approach to this line is suggested by Wang Lijia in an article on *pu*, simplicity. He interprets the focusing of eyes and ears as acts of sensory acquisition based on desire, and the sage's "parenting" of the people as returning them to desireless simplicity. See "Lun Laozi de *pu* zhi sixiang" in *Guanzi xuekan* 1998.3, p. 81.

3. The entire "Dark Robes" is also a chapter in the *Liji*, or *Book of Rituals*.

4. The opening line of this stanza resembles a key line in Sunzi's *Art of War*: "Those who have the Way cause the people to have the same mind as their superiors" (*Sunzi bingfa*, "Jipian"). Sunzi applies many of the ideas from the *Laozi*, but his overall view of war is the opposite of Laozi's. Sunzi is purely exploitative—"gain power through advantage"—and has no interest in the antimilitarist aspects of Daoist thought.

5. In the Mawangdui text, the word *hai*, child-in-embrace, is written in a variant way that yields the meaning *he*, exclude. In that case, the final image is the rejection of the senses of seeing and hearing, rather than an all-embracing nonjudgmental mother. It seems to me that the latter, with its ironic spin on the Confucian model of patriarch as the ruler of his children-subjects, is a preferable reading.

STANZA 50

1. *Shesheng* in line 9—"secret oneself" or "protect life"—is a unique phrase for this text. *Shesheng* is often equated with *yangsheng*, to nourish or preserve life. The meaning of *she* is to safeguard something by secreting it away *(cang)*, to draw it into something else or into itself for protection so that it can be kept whole for later use. The Mawangdui text, however, has instead *zhi* (maintain, hold on to), a reading that fits better with the alternative translation at the end of the comment "keep himself whole."

2. A comparable passage occurs in the "Neiye" chapter of the *Guanzi*: "If you can maintain oneness and discard ten thousand burdens, see advantage and not be tempted, danger and not take fright. . . ."

3. Burton Watson, "Mastering Life" ("Dasheng"), *The Complete Works of Chuang Tzu*, pp. 198–99. I have slightly altered Watson's translation. For further information on textual variations, see Robert Henricks, *Lao-tzu Te-Tao Ching*, p. 122.

STANZA 51

1. The unusual grammatical pattern in lines 1–4 and lines 10–15, verb + *zhi* (direct object) repeated several times, is found in the chapter "Zheng" (Correctness in rule) of the *Guanzi*. This stanza is not in the Guodian text.

STANZA 52

1. *Huainanzi*, "Jingshen," p. 322.

2. Only lines 8–13 of this stanza are found in the Guodian manuscript, where, however, they are in reverse order, with lines 11–13 preceding

lines 8–10. Thus, if lines 1–7 and 14–19 are unconnected, there may be three stanzas combined in this one.

STANZA 53

1. In this translation *chu* is taken as "enjoy a blessing," as in the *Shijing* ode "Tianbao."

2. Burton Watson, *The Complete Works of Chuang Tzu*, p. 110.

STANZA 54

1. *Guanzi,* "Mumin" (Guiding the people).

STANZA 55

1. In line 8 the present translation follows the Heshang gong commentary, which unlike other texts includes the Guodian graph *nu,* aroused (phallus), in its explanation. This stanza is found in the Guodian text.

2. The Guodian text reads: "It spends the whole day without distress."

3. In the Guodian manuscript "knowing" is not found in line 11.

4. Cited in Jiao Hong, *Laozi yi.*

5. Burton Watson, *The Complete Works of Chuang Tzu*, p. 253.

6. Burton Watson, *The Complete Works of Chuang Tzu*, p. 58.

STANZA 56

1. Lines 3–7, which also appear in stanza 4, have been excised from stanza 4 in this translation. They may be a separate stanza from either stanza 4 or stanza 56.

2. Burton Watson, *The Complete Works of Chuang Tzu*, p. 111.

STANZA 57

1. According to the Guodian and Mawangdui texts, line 6 reads "the more the people will violate them"; this reading seems to make better sense than "deprived." Compare Mozi's argument that rituals are injurious economically. Also *Analects* 6.25, where the word *pan* (rebel) means violation of ritual. "Deprived" and "violate" are phonetically similar, both being within the phoneme **pwan.*

2. The noted modern Laozi scholar Chen Guying sees in lines 14–21, which advocate protection of the autonomy and productivity of the common people, "a spiritual need for freedom and democracy in ancient times" ("Daojia zai xian Qin zhexueshi shang de zhugan diwei," in *Daojia wenhua yanjiu,* no. 10, p. 24).

See Gu Li and Zhou Ying, *Laozi tong,* 2: 117, for a list of *Zuozhuan* illustrations of increasing laws and regulations in the Spring and Autumn period.

3. *Jingfa,* "Daofa." See Bai Xi, *Jixia xue yanjiu,* p. 121, for analysis of the compatibility of law and *Dao.*

STANZA 58

1. An alternative reading of lines 1 and 2 is: "Under rule that shows concern / The people are simple and stolid."

2. "Shed light" in line 17 is the translation of *guang,* which seems to refer to the light of both the sun and moon, and also, by analogy, to the understanding of the eye and ear *(yu ri yue can qi guang),* which could be generalized to the "powers of the mind." *Guang* is translated as "points of view" in stanza 56.

3. Burton Watson, *The Complete Works of Chuang Tzu,* p. 253. "Embrace the one" is *baoyi.*

4. Gu Li and Zhou Ying, *Laozi tong,* 1:203.

STANZA 59

1. The Guodian text has the word *bei,* prepared, not *fu,* submit. The word is translated "precaution." The meaning is that the provisions necessary for governing and for sacrifices would be ready and abundant beforehand. This agricultural orientation may explain the hostility to crafts and commerce expressed in other stanzas. Following the Han Feizi view that *se* means storing up virtue, Su Che says, "To have but not use defines *se.*" The present translation accepts *bei* over *fu;* Karlgren's archaic reconstructed pronunciations are **b'ieg* and **b'iuk.* Note that **b'iuk* is a homophone for "abundance," "wealth" (the modern *fu*).

2. *Ji,* "turning point" or "limit," means the boundary between *yin* and *yang* or between opposites.

3. In line 16 the word *shi* (focus the sight, examine), consistent in all texts, can be taken either as a reference to sustained concentration (during a long life) or else as the phonetically related word *li,* remain in position. Then "extended life" would be the result of personal discipline, and remaining in position would be the result of political control. This reading combines the themes of governance and personal cultivation.

4. See Yin Zhenhuan's article "*Laozi Guanzi de yi jiqi fazhan,*" *Guanzi xuekan* 1991.3, pp. 16–22; see also his comment on the penultimate line of this stanza in "*Boshu Laozi hanyi butong de wenju,*" *Daojia wenhua yanjiu* 10, p. 149.

STANZA 60

1. Burton Watson, *The Complete Works of Chuang Tzu*, p. 172.

STANZA 61

1. Gu Li and Zhou Ying, *Laozi tong*, 1:535–36.

STANZA 62

1. There is no Guodian text for this stanza. The Mawangdui text has *zhi* instead of *ao* (midden, sacred disposal site). *Zhu*, water flowing toward, picks up the imagery of the preceding stanza. Line 1 would then mean that the Way is the point toward which all ten thousand stream. "Men of merit" probably refers to those who offer proper counsel to the king.

2. In line 5 this translation follows the Mawangdui text, which has *he*, congratulate, instead of *jia*, impose. The meaning is not obvious. Perhaps *he* is causative: "win men's praises." If *jia* is accepted as the reading, then the line would mean "fine deeds overawe others." Even before the Mawangdui discovery translators accepted *he* over *jia*, based on two supporting citations in the *Huainanzi*.

STANZA 63

1. This famous line, line 5, also found in the *Analects*, is not in the Guodian text. Some believe it has no connection with this text and could have been added to tie the *Laozi* to the *Analects*. But it seems intelligible in the context. And perhaps another ancient version of this stanza included this line.

The preceding line, line 4, reads only "what is great is to be made small" in the Guodian text. The companion phrase, "what is much should be made less" is not included. While the syntactical indeterminacy of the Mawangdui and standard texts permits the reverse reading commonly adopted in translation—treat the small as great—clearly the reading "make the great small" accords better with the "less is more" philosophy of this stanza and other stanzas as well.

2. As for the non-Guodian lines, it looks as if material from stanza 64 has been incorporated into stanza 63. Yin Zhenhuan in his *Boshu Laozi* suggests that there are three stanzas here: lines 1–5, 6–11, and 12–15.

STANZA 64

1. In line 1 the Guodian text uses an ancient variant for *kun* (contain, imprison) instead of *chi* (to secure); in that case the sense of the line may be:

"What is in a fixed position is easy to contain." In line 2, *weizhao,* not yet manifest, may also mean "before the divination cracks appear," that is, before the die is cast, before the line is drawn.

2. If "learn" is causative, line 27 means "teach what others do not teach."

3. *Han Feizi,* "Yu Lao." Han Feizi's anecdote suggests that Laozi directed his advice to lords and their ministers. The ambiguity of the syntax allows another reading for lines 25 and 27: "desire not to desire" and "learn not to learn" (or "teach not to teach"), respectively.

4. For a discussion of Laozi's influence on the early *Guanzi* chapters, see Hu Jiacong, *Guanzi xintan,* pp. 211–15.

5. See Gao Chenyang, "Guodian Chujian *Laozi* de zhenxiang jiqi yu jinben *Laozi* de guanxi," *Zhongguo zhexue shi,* 1999.3, p. 81. This article was written in response to Guo Qi's article in *Zhexue yanjiu* 1998.7, which argues that the Guodian manuscript is an earlier, superior text to the received text.

6. See Yin Zhenhuan, "Huifu *Laozi* de benlai mianmu" in *Wenxian* 1992.3. In *Boshu Laozi shixi* Yin Zhenhuan proposes splitting this stanza into five independent ones comprised of lines 1–6, 7–13, 14–18, 19–23, and 24–31.

STANZA 66

1. In the Guodian text line 6 has no *yu,* "wishing." Adding the *yu* suggests a more manipulative ruler. Without *yu,* the ruler simply behaves humbly without calculation. See Guo Qi, "Chujian 'Laozi' yu Laozi gong'an," in *Guodian Chujian yanjiu,* ed. Jiang Kuanghui, Zhongguo zhexue, no. 20. The word *shan* (knowing how to, skilled at) in line 3 supports the inclusion of *yu* and the idea that the ruler cunningly rather than naturally subordinates himself.

2. The word *hai* (threat, harm) in line 11 may be a simplified version of a similar graph *xian,* meaning laws, models, and institutions. If so, this line would then mean that such a leader imposes no conformity.

STANZA 67

1. "Triple treasure" *(sanbao)* in line 7 is also mentioned in *Mencius* 7B.28: "The feudal lords have three treasures: their land, their people, their administration. Disaster will overtake whoever treasures jewels and gems."

2. *Jiu* means to save, keep; in the Mawangdui text we find *jian* (to sustain in power, to establish).

3. In Gu Li's view, the phrase *qizhang,* sacred elder of the world, in line 12 suggests a Spring and Autumn date for the text (*Laozi tong,* 1:566).

STANZA 69

1. A number of scholars have said that the *gu*, olden, in the last line of the previous stanza really belongs to the first line of this one: "In olden times those who waged war. . . ."

2. Do lines 4–7 refer to the offensive side, the host side, or the defensive side, the guest side? Most commentaries and translations assume the latter, but Gu Li takes the lines to refer to the attackers: "If they march but have no where to march / Or arm to raise [to summon a host] / Or weapon to take in hand / Or opponent to go for" (Gu Li and Zhou Ying, *Laozi tong*, 1:577–78). For line 7, Yin Zhenhuan adopts the Mawangdui text: *nai wu di* rather than *reng wu di*: "And thus there is no encounter."

3. *Huangdi sijing*, p. 129; Bai Xi, *Jixia xue yanjiu*, p. 119.

STANZA 70

1. The unusual application of the term "ancestral" to a philosophical formula in line 5 is also found in the *Guanzi*: "Filial devotion and fraternal love are the *zu* (grandfather) of *ren* (humanity)" ("Jie"); "Take inner quiet as *zong* (ancestor) and timeliness as treasure" ("Baixin").

STANZA 71

1. Lines 1 and 2 are basically the same in all versions, but the sentences that follow are in different order in different texts. The general sense does not seem to change, however. I have used Chen Guying's arrangement here (*Laozi zhuyi ji pingjie*).

2. See Jiao Hong, *Laozi yi*.

STANZA 72

1. Gu Li and Zhou Ying, *Laozi tong*, 2:529–31.

2. *Zuozhuan*, Zhaogong 20.

STANZA 73

1. Yin Zhenhuan gives lines 1–5 a rather legalistic reading:

1   Those bold in daring, let them be killed;
2   Those bold in not daring, let them be spared;
3   One of these two brings gain, one harm.
4   What Heaven condemns, who knows the reason?
5   Even the wise are troubled.

This reading follows the Heshang gong and Yan Zun commentaries. Yan Zun says that severity and mercy are both needed by the ruler.

2. Many editions have *mo* (keep silent) in place of *dan* (unaffected, disengaged) in line 10.

3. Jiao Hong, *Laozi yi.*

STANZA 74

1. Line 6 is inserted from the Mawangdui text.

2. Both the *Wenzi* ("Shangren") and the Yan Zun commentary see this stanza arguing for separation of functions between ruler and minister; heaven is not in the picture at all. An analysis of this stanza may be found in Guo Shiming's "Boshu *Laozi* sanduan ling shi," *Beijing daxue xuebao* (zhexue shehui kexue ban) 1997.5.

3. Xu Xiaotian, *Laozi gailun* (1930; reprint, Beijing: Zhongguo shudian, 1988).

STANZA 75

1. The Mawangdui text has no *shang* ("those above") in line 5. The customary reading of this line depends on inserting the subject *shang:* "those in power live a life too rich." Perhaps this word was added to coordinate the two otherwise independent halves of this stanza.

2. Sunzi, *Art of War*, "Zuozhan" (Waging war).

STANZA 77

1. Jiao Hong, *Laozi yi.*

STANZA 78

1. Gu Li and Zhou Ying, *Laozi tong,* 1:170. See also Jiao Hong, *Laozi yi.* Stanzas like this one probably were in the mind of the third-century B.C. philosopher and historian of philosophy Xunzi when he said that Laozi "failed to distinguish the noble from the mean" (*Xunzi*, "Tiandao").

2. Gao Heng, *Chongding Laozi zhenggu.* See also Jiao Hong, *Laozi yi.* Yin Zhenhuan cites the well-known *Guanzi* passage: "The wise king takes the fault upon himself when he goes wrong, while he ascribes all successes to the people" ("Xiaocheng").

STANZA 79

1. *Chunqiu fanlu,* "Zhulin."

STANZA 80

1. Burton Watson, *The Complete Works of Chuang Tzu*, pp. 111–12.

2. Judging from the Mencius passage, "echoing cries of cocks and dogs" was probably a common saying in the kingdom of Qi.

STANZA 81

1. For the argument and supporting quotes see Yin Zhenhuan, "Huifu *Laozi* de benlai mianmu," *Wenxian* 1998.1, pp. 77–78. In the Mawangdui text the couplets in lines 3–4 and lines 5–6 occur in reverse order. The text of lines 3–4 also differs: *shanzhe bu duo / duozhe bushan,* "The good [in power, in office] are few / The majority are not good."

SELECTED BIBLIOGRAPHY

CHINESE

Primary Sources

Chen Guying, ed. *Zhuangzi jinzhu jinyi*. Beijing: Zhonghua shuju. 1983; reprinted 1991.

Chen Qiyou, ed. *Han Feizi jishi*. Shanghai: Shanghai renmin chubanshe, 1974.

Chen Yiping, ed. *Huainanzi jiao, zhu, yi*. Guangzhou: Guangdong renmin chubanshe, 1994.

Chen Zizhan et al., eds. *Shijing zhijie*. Shanghai: Fudan daxue chubanshe, 1983.

Cui Renyi, ed. *Jingmen Guodian Chujian Laozi yanjiu*. Beijing: Kexue chubanshe, 1998.

Guo Moruo et al., eds. *Guanzi jijiao*. Beijing: Kexue chubanshe, 1956.

Heshang gong. *Laozi Daodejing Heshang gong zhangju*. Beijing: Zhonghua shuju, 1993.

Jiang Hao et al., eds. *Jinguwen Shangshu quanyi*. Guiyang: Guizhou renmin chubanshe, 1990.

Jingmenshi bowuguan, eds. *Guodian Chumu zhujian*. Beijing: Wenwu chubanshe, 1998.

Legge, James, trans. *Confucian Analects, The Great Learning, and The Doctrine of the Mean*. Chinese Classics Series, vol. 1. Oxford: Clarendon Press, 1893.

———. *The Works of Mencius*. Chinese Classics Series, vol. 2. Oxford: Clarendon Press, 1895.

Li Dingsheng and Xu Huijun, eds. *Wenzi yaoquan*. Shanghai: Fudan daxue chubanshe, 1988.

Rao Zongyi, ed. *Laozi Xiang'erzhu jiaozheng*. Shanghai: Shanghai guji chubanshe, 1991.

Wang Bi. *Laozi zhu*. Shanghai: Shanghai guji chubanshe, 1993.

Wang Meng'ou, ed. *Liji jinzhu jinyi*. Tianjin: Tianjin guji chubanshe, 1983.

Wang Pinzhen, ed. *Da Dai Liji jiegu*. Beijing: Zhonghua shuju, 1983.

Wang Shouqian et al., ed. *Zuozhuan quanyi*. Guiyang: Guizhou renmin chubanshe, 1990.

———. *Zhanguoce quanyi*. Guiyang: Guizhou renmin chubanshe, 1992.

Wu Shundong et al., eds. *Shiji quanyi*. 4 vols. Guiyang: Guizhou renmin chubanshe, 1990.

Xu Kangsheng, ed. *Boshu Laozi zhuyi yu yanjiu*. Rev. ed. Hangzhou: Zhejiang renmin chubanshe, 1985.

Xunzi, Beijing daxue Xunzi zhushizu, eds. *Xunzi xinzhu*. Beijing: Zhonghua shuju, 1979.

Yan Zun. *Laozi zhigui*. Beijing: Zhongguo shuju, 1994.

Yu Mingguang, ed. *Huangdi sijing jinzhu jinyi*. Changsha: Yuelu shushe, 1993.

Zhang Zhenze, ed. *Sun Bin bingfa jiaoli*. Beijing: Zhonghua shuju, 1984.

Secondary Sources

Bai Xi. *Jixia xue yanjiu*. Beijing: Sanlian shudian, 1998.

Chen Guying. *Lao-Zhuang xinlun*. Shanghai: Shanghai guji chubanshe, 1992.

———, ed. *Laozi zhuyi ji pingjie*. Hong Kong: Zhonghua shuju, 1987.

———. *Daojia wenhua yanjiu*. Shanghai: Shanghai guji chubanshe, 1992–.

This ongoing series now contains seventeen volumes. It is an invaluable collection of learned articles by Chinese and foreign scholars from all over the world, devoted to every aspect of Daoist thought, history, texts, and commentary.

Ding Yuanming. *Huang-Lao xue lungang*. Shandong daxue chubanshe, 1997.

Gao Heng, ed. *Chongding Laozi zhenggu*. Beijing: Zhonghua shuju, 1956.

Gu Li and Zhou Ying. *Laozi tong*. 2 vols. Changchun: Jilin renmin chuban she, 1991.

Hu Jiacong. *Guanzi xintan*. Beijing: Zhongguo shehui kexue chubanshe, 1995.

———. *Jixia zhengming yu Huang-Lao xinxue*. Beijing: Zhongguo shehui kexue chubanshe, 1998.

Jiang Kuanghui, ed. *Guodian Chujian yanjiu*. Zhongguo zhexue, no. 20. Shenyang: Liaoning jiaoyu chubanshe, 1999.

Jiang Xichang, ed. *Laozi jiaogu*. Commercial Press, 1937; reprint, Chengdu: Chengdu guji shudian, 1988.

Jiao Hong, comp. *Laozi yi*. 1895; reprint, Taibei: Guangwen shuju, 1962.

Li Gang. *Handai Daojiao zhexue*. Chengdu: Ba-Shu shushe, 1992.

Liu Huihua and Miao Runtian. *Jixia xueshi*. Beijing: Zhongguo guangbo dianshi chubanshe, 1992.

Na Wei. *Handai Daojia de zhengzhi sixiang he zhijue tiwu*. Jinan: Qi-Lu shushe, 1992.

Peng Hao, ed. *Guodian Chujian Laozi jiaodu*. Wuhan: Hubei renmin chubanshe, 2000.

Sha Shaohai and Xu Zihong, eds. *Laozi quanyi*. Guiyang: Guizhou renmin chubanshe, 1989.

Wang Li. *Laozi yanjiu*. Shanghai: Commercial Press, 1928.

Wei Yuan, ed. *Laozi benyi*. Taipei: Shijie shuju, 1949.

Yin Zhenhuan, ed. *Boshu Laozi shixi*. Guiyang: Guizhou renmin chubanshe, 1998.

Zhang Songru, ed. *Laozi jiaodu*. Changchun: Jilin renmin chubanshe, 1981.

Zhao Jibin. *Kunzhi erlu*. Beijing: Zhonghuo shuju, 1991.

Zhu Qianzhi, ed. *Laozi jiaoshi*. 1954. Reprint Zhonghua shuju, 1996.

ENGLISH

Bokenkamp, Stephen R. *Early Daoist Scriptures*. Berkeley: University of California Press, 1997.

Chan, Alan K. L. *Two Visions of the Way: A Study of the Wang Pi and Ho-shang Kung Commentaries on the Lao-Tzu*. Albany: State University of New York Press, 1991.

Chan, Wing-Tsit. *The Way of Lao Tzu*. Indianapolis and New York: Bobbs-Merrill, 1963.

Hawkes, David. *Ch'u Tz'u: The Songs of the South*. Oxford: Clarendon Press, 1959.

Henricks, Robert. *Lao-Tzu Te-Tao Ching: A New Translation Based on the Recently Discovered Ma-wang-tui Texts*. New York: Ballantine, 1989.

———. *Lao Tzu's Tao Te Ching: A Translation of the Startling New Documents Found at Guodian*. New York: Columbia University Press, 2000.

Kohn, Livia, and Michael LaFargue. *Lao-Tzu and the Tao-de-ching*. Albany: State University of New York Press, 1998.

Lao, D. C. *Tao Te Ching*. New York: Knopf, 1994.

Lin Wusun, trans. *Sunzi: The Art of War; Sun Bin: The Art of War*. Bilingual edition. Beijing: People's China Publishing House, 1995.

Loewe, Michael, and Edward L. Shaughnessy. *The Cambridge History of Ancient China*. Cambridge: Cambridge University Press, 1999.

Lynn, Richard. *The Classic of the Way and Virtue*. New York: Columbia University Press, 1999.

Mair, Victor. *Tao Te Ching: The Classic Book of Integrity and the Way*. New York: Bantam Books, 1990.

Rickett, W. Allyn. *Guanzi: Political, Economic, and Philosophical Essays from*

Early China: A Study and Translation. 2 vols. Princeton: Princeton University Press, 1985, 1998.

Waley, Arthur. *The Way and Its Power.* Allen & Unwin, 1934; reprint, New York: Grove Press, 1958.

———. *The Book of Songs.* 1937; reprint, New York: Grove Press, 1960.

Watson, Burton. *Mo Tzu: Basic Writings.* New York and London: Columbia University Press, 1963.

———. *The Complete Works of Chuang Tzu.* New York: Columbia University Press, 1968.

Yates, Robin D. S. *Five Lost Classics: Tao, Huang-Lao, and Yin-Yang in Han China.* New York: Ballantine, Del Rey Fawcett, 1997.

Designer:	Barbara Jellow
Compositor:	G&S Typesetters, Inc.
Text:	Dante
Display:	Cochin/Cochin Italic
Printer & Binder:	Haddon Craftsmen